D0181850

Why Trust the Bible?

ONLY IF YOU ARE
A CHRISTIAN

ROSE
PUBLISHING

Torrance, California

© 2008 Bristol Works, Inc.
Rose Publishing, Inc.
4733 Torrance Blvd., #259
Torrance, California 90503 U.S.A.
Email: info@rose-publishing.com
www.rose-publishing.com

Free, downloadable study guide at rose-publishing.com. Click on "News & Info," then on "Downloads."

Includes these Rose Publishing Titles:

How We Got the Bible © 2005, 2007, 2008 RW Research, Inc.
    Contributors: Philip W. Comfort, PhD; Errol F. Rhodes; John McRay, PhD;
    Lawrence Scrivani; Michael Cochrane, MA
Dead Sea Scrolls © 2005 World of the Bible Ministries
    Author: J. Randall Price, PhD
50 Proofs: Old Testament © 2007 RW Research, Inc.
    Contributors: Larry McKinney; Dan Master; John Monson, PhD
50 Proofs: New Testament © 2007 RW Research, Inc.
    Contributors: Larry McKinney; John McRay; Michael Cochrane, MA
Why Trust the Bible? © 2007 Bristol Works, Inc.
    Author: Timothy Paul Jones, EdD
100 Prophecies Fulfilled by Jesus © 2002, 2005 RW Research, Inc.
    Contributors: G. Goldsmith, Carol R. Witte
The Gospels: "Lost" & Found © 2007 Bristol Works, Inc.
    Author: Timothy Paul Jones, EdD
Many of these titles are available as individual pamphlets, as wall charts, and as ready-to-use PowerPoint® presentations.

Library of Congress Cataloging-in-Publication Data

Why trust the Bible?
    p. cm. – (Rose Bible basics)
  ISBN 978-1-59636-201-7 (pbk.)
  1. Bible–Evidences, authority, etc. I. Rose Publishing (Torrance, Calif.)
  BS480.W4897 2008
  220.1–dc22

                          2008007519

Printed in China
010308RRD

WHY TRUST THE BIBLE?

Contents

Continued
on next
page
→

WHY TRUST
THE BIBLE?

Contents

How We Got
the Bible

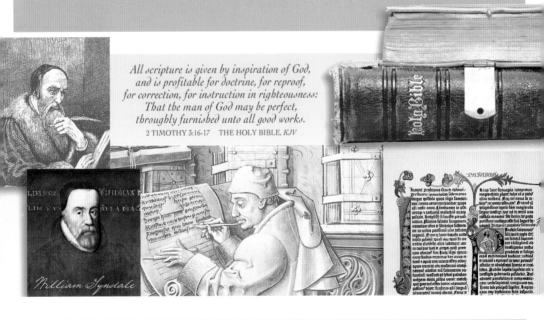

*All scripture is given by inspiration of God,
and is profitable for doctrine, for reproof,
for correction, for instruction in righteousness:
That the man of God may be perfect,
throughly furnished unto all good works.*

2 TIMOTHY 3:16-17   THE HOLY BIBLE, *KJV*

William Tyndale

A Time Line of Key Events in the
History of the Bible

How We Got the Bible
Ten Key Points

1 The Bible is inspired by God (2 Timothy 3:16-17; 2 Peter 1:20-21).

2 The Bible is made up of 66 different books that were written over 1600 years (from approximately 1500 BC to AD 100) by more than 40 kings, prophets, leaders, and followers of Jesus. The Old Testament has 39 books (written approximately 1500-400 BC). The New Testament has 27 books (written approximately AD 45-100). The Hebrew Bible has the same text as the English Bible's Old Testament, but divides and arranges it differently.

3 The Old Testament was written mainly in Hebrew, with some Aramaic. The New Testament was written in Greek.

4 The books of the Bible were collected and arranged and recognized as inspired sacred authority by councils of rabbis and councils of church leaders based on careful guidelines.

5 Before the printing press was invented, the Bible was copied by hand. The Bible was copied very accurately, in many cases by special scribes who developed intricate methods of counting words and letters to insure that no errors had been made.

6 The Bible was the first book ever printed on the printing press with moveable type (Gutenberg Press, 1455, Latin Bible).

7 There is much evidence that the Bible we have today is remarkably true to the original writings. Of the thousands of copies made by hand before 1500, more than 5,300 Greek manuscripts from the New Testament alone still exist today. The text of the Bible is better preserved than the writings of Plato or Aristotle.

8 The discovery of the Dead Sea Scrolls confirmed the astonishing reliability of some of the copies of the Old Testament made over the years. Although some spelling variations exist, no variation affects basic Bible doctrines.

9 As the Bible was carried to other countries, it was translated into the common language of the people by scholars who wanted others to know God's Word. Today there are still 2,000 groups with no Bible in their own language.

10 By AD 200, the Bible was translated into seven languages; by 500, 13 languages; by 900, 17 languages; by 1400, 28 languages; by 1800, 57 languages; by 1900, 537 languages; by 1980, 1,100 languages; by 2006, 2,426 languages have some portions of the Scripture.

Source: *The World Christian Encyclopedia*; Wycliffe, International.

Old Testament Written (approx. 1500-400 BC)

stone

clay

leather

New Testament Written (approx. AD 45-100)

papyrus

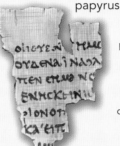

The oldest New Testament fragment (from John 18) that we have today was copied in Greek on a papyrus codex around AD 110-130.

Bible Copied on Papyrus

Scrolls of leather, and later of papyrus, were used to make copies of the Scriptures.

A papyrus *codex* is a bound volume made from sheets folded and sewn together, sometimes with a cover. They were used more than scrolls after AD 1-100.

Bible Copied on Fine Animal Skins

Fine quality animal skins from calves or antelope (vellum) and sheep or goats (parchment) were used for over 1000 years to make copies of the Bible approximately AD 300-1400.

Two of the oldest vellum copies (AD 325-350) that exist today are the Vatican Codex and the Sinaitic Codex.

Bible Printed by Printing Press after 1455

Wycliffe Bibles were inscribed by hand on vellum in the 1300s-1400s. Some copies took ten months to two years to produce and cost a year's wage.

The Bible was the first book to be printed with Gutenberg's printing press in 1455.

The Bible, God's Word to the World

The Bible is now printed on paper in many versions and languages. It is also on recordings and the Internet.

2000 BC   500 BC   200 BC

Old Testament events are written down in Hebrew (portions in Aramaic) over centuries. In Exodus, the Lord tells Moses to write in a book. Other Old Testament writers, inspired by God, include leaders, kings and prophets. Together, these writings on leather scrolls and other materials are called the Hebrew Scriptures or Old Testament.

Ezra, a priest and scribe, collects and arranges some of the books of the Hebrew Bible—the Old Testament—about 450 BC, according to Jewish tradition.

The Septuagint is the Greek translation of the Hebrew Bible (the Old Testament). It is translated in 250-100 BC by Jewish scholars in Alexandria, Egypt. (The word *Septuagint* means seventy, referring to the tradition that 70 or 72 men translated it. It is often abbreviated LXX, the Roman numeral for seventy.)

The books are arranged by subject: historical, poetic, and prophetic. It includes the Apocrypha (meaning "hidden"), referring to seven books that were included in the Hebrew Bible until AD 90 when they were removed by Jewish elders.

A Scribe

AD 100   AD 200

Followers of Jesus

Matthew, Mark, Luke, John, Paul, James, Peter, and Jude write the Gospels, history, letters to other Christians, and the Revelation between AD 45 and 100. The writers quote from all but eight of the Old Testament books. These writings in Greek are copied and circulated so that by about 150 there is wide enough use of them to speak of the "New Testament" ("New Covenant"). The new covenant God made with people was promised in Jer. 31:31-34 and referred to by Jesus (Luke 22:20) and Paul (1 Cor. 11:25) and in the letter to the Hebrews.

Early Coptic Translation

Old Testament Apocrypha

Evidence derived from first century AD writers Philo and Josephus indicates that the Hebrew canon did not include the Apocrypha.

Earliest Translations

200-300 Latin, Coptic (Egypt), and Syriac (Syria).

Church Fathers accept

the writings of the Gospels and Paul's letters as *canonical* (from a Greek word referring to the *rule* of faith and truth). Origen lists 21 approved New Testament books. Eusebius lists 22 accepted books.

AD 1

Papyrus, a plant, is cut into strips and pressed into sheets of writing material and can be made into a scroll or a codex. The New Testament books were probably first written on papyrus scrolls. Later Christians begin to copy them on sheets of papyrus which are bound and placed between two pieces of wood for covers. This form of early book is known as a codex.

Papyrus

Time of Jesus
4 BC-AD 33?

Jesus quotes the Old Testament (Scriptures) often. He says that He did not come to destroy the Scriptures, but to fulfill them. He says to his disciples, "These are the words which I spake unto you, . . . that all things must be fulfilled, which were written in the law of Moses, and in the prophets, and in the psalms, concerning me. Then opened he their understanding, that they might understand the scriptures." Luke 24:44-45

AD 300

Saint Matthew
Lindisfarne Gospels
Approximately 900

The New Testament books are collected and circulated throughout the Mediterranean about the time of Constantine, the Roman emperor who legalizes Christianity in 313. By 400 the standard of 27 New Testament books is accepted in the East and West as confirmed by Athanasius, Jerome, Augustine and three church councils. The 27 books of the New Testament were formally confirmed as canonical by the Synod of Carthage in 397, thus recognizing three centuries of use by followers of Christ.

Jerome starts translating the Scriptures into Latin in 410 and finishes 25 years later. This translation, called the Latin Vulgate, remains the basic Bible for many centuries.

Jerome

AD 500

Roman Empire declines. Germanic migrations (378-600) cause new languages to emerge.

The Masoretes are special Jewish scribes entrusted with the sacred task of making copies of the Hebrew Scriptures (Old Testament) approximately 500-900. They develop a meticulous system of counting the number of words in each book of the Bible to make sure they have copied it accurately. Any scroll found to have an error is buried according to Jewish law.

AD 600

Christianity reaches Britain before 300, but Anglo-Saxon pagans drive Christian Britons into Wales (450-600). In 596, Augustine of Canterbury begins evangelization again.

Caedmon, an illiterate monk, retells portions of Scripture in Anglo-Saxon (Old English) poetry and song (676).

Aldhelm of Sherborne, 709, is said to have translated the Psalms.

Bede

Bede, a monk and scholar, makes an Old English (Anglo-Saxon) translation of portions of Scripture. On his deathbed in 735, he finishes translating the Book of John.

AD 1400

In 1408, in England, it becomes illegal to translate or read the Bible in common English without permission of a bishop.

World's first printing press with moveable metal type is invented in 1455 in Germany by Johann Gutenberg. This invention is perhaps the single most important event to influence the spread of the Bible.

The Gutenberg Bible is the first book ever printed. This Latin Vulgate version is often illuminated by artists who hand paint letters and ornaments on each page.

Gutenberg Bible Page

Erasmus, a priest and Greek scholar, publishes a new Greek edition and a more accurate Latin translation of the New Testament in 1516. His goal is that everyone be able to read the Bible, from the farmer in the field to the weaver at the loom. Erasmus' Greek text forms the basis of the *"textus receptus"* and is used later by Martin Luther, William Tyndale, and the King James translators.

AD 1300

Alfred The Great, King of Wessex (871-901) translates portions of Exodus, Psalms, and Acts.

Aldred, Bishop of Durham, inserts a translation in the Northumbrian dialect between the lines of the Lindisfarne Gospels (950).

Aelfric (955-1020) translates portions of the Old Testament.

Normans conquer England (1066) and make French the official language. No English translation work produced until the 1300s.

Middle English emerges, popularized by works such as the *Canterbury Tales* and Richard Rolle's *Psalter* (1340).

John Wycliffe

First English Bible is translated from Latin in 1382 and is called the Wycliffe Bible in honor of priest and Oxford scholar John Wycliffe. During his lifetime, Wycliffe had wanted common people to have the Bible. He also criticized a number of church practices and policies. His followers, derisively called Lollards (meaning "mumblers"), included his criticisms in the preface to the Wycliffe Bible. This Bible is banned and burned. Forty years after Wycliffe's death, his bones are exhumed and burned for heresy.

AD 1500

Erasmus

Martin Luther translates the New Testament into German in 1522.

William Tyndale, priest and Oxford scholar, translates the New Testament from Greek (1525), but cannot get approval to publish it in England. He moves to Germany and prints Bibles, smuggling them into England in sacks of corn and flour. In 1535 he publishes part of the Old Testament translated from Hebrew. In 1536, Tyndale is strangled and burned at the stake. His final words are "Lord, open the King of England's eyes."

Tyndale is called the "Father of the English Bible" because his translation forms the basis of the King James Version. Much of the style and vocabulary we know as "biblical English" is traceable to his work.

William Tyndale

AD 1500

The Coverdale Bible

is translated by Miles Coverdale (1535) and dedicated to Anne Boleyn, one of King Henry VIII's wives. This is the first complete Bible to be printed in English.

Tyndale's Initials
printed in the
Matthew's Bible

The Matthew's Bible,

translated by John Rogers under the pen name "Thomas Matthew," is the first Bible published with the king's permission (1537). Printed just one year after Tyndale's death, its New Testament relies heavily on Tyndale's version, and even has a tribute to him on the last page of the Old Testament. Tyndale's initials are printed in 2½-inch block letters. Later Thomas Cromwell, advisor to King Henry VIII, entrusts Coverdale to revise Matthew's Bible to make the Great Bible.

The Great Bible (1539)

is placed in every church by order of Thomas Cranmer, archbishop under King Henry VIII. This Bible is chained to the church pillars to discourage theft.

The "Chained Bible"

AD 1600

King James Bible
Page from 1611 version

King James Version or Authorized Version

King James I of England commissions 54 scholars to undertake a new Bible translation. Over the next six years, six teams of scholars using the Bishops Bible and Tyndale's Bible, as well as available Greek and Hebrew manuscripts, complete the new version in 1611. The King James Version (also called the "Authorized Version," even though King James never gave the finished version his royal approval) is revised several times.

(The edition used today was revised in 1769.) It is the most popular Bible for more than 300 years.

King James

AD 1555

England's Queen Mary bans Protestant translations of the English Bible. John Rogers and Thomas Cranmer are burned at the stake. Later some 300 men, women and children are also burned.

The Geneva Bible

Exiles from England flee to Geneva, Switzerland, and in 1560 print the Geneva Bible, a complete revision of the Great Bible with the Old Testament translated from Hebrew. The Geneva Bible contains theological notes from Protestant scholars John Calvin, Beza, Knox, and Whittingham. It is the first Bible to use Roman type instead of black letter. This is the Bible of Shakespeare and the one carried to America by the Pilgrims in 1620. The 1640 edition is the first English Bible to omit the Apocrypha.

Queen Mary

Bishops Bible

A new translation begins under Queen Elizabeth in 1568. It is translated by several bishops of the Church of England in answer to the Geneva Bible.

Rheims-Douai Bible

was translated into English from the Latin Vulgate by Catholic scholar Gregory Martin, while in exile in France (New Testament in 1582/Old Testament in 1609). It becomes the standard translation for the Catholic church.

AD 1800

Older Manuscripts Discovered!
Between 1629 and 1947, several of the earliest known copies of the Bible are found.

Codex Alexandrinus,
a copy of the New Testament from 400, perhaps the best copy of the book of Revelation, is made available to western scholars in 1629.

Codex Sinaiticus
(earliest complete copy of the New Testament, copied in 350) is found in St. Catherine's Monastery near Mt. Sinai.

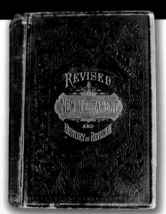

The Revised Version

The Revised Version
(1885) In 1870, scholars in England decide to revise the King James Version to reflect the findings from the manuscripts discovered during the two previous centuries. Their goal is to use better Hebrew and Greek texts and to retranslate words based on new linguistic information about ancient Hebrew.

Codex Vaticanus
(earliest and probably best copy known of the New Testament from 325) is released to scholars in 1889 by the Vatican Library.

AD 1900

The Dead Sea Scrolls, found in a cave in 1947 by a shepherd, contain the oldest known copies of portions of the Old Testament. These copies were made between 100 BC and AD 100.

A Qumran Cave near the Dead Sea

A Scroll of Isaiah that is part of the Dead Sea Scrolls is the oldest complete manuscript of any book of the Bible (copied around 100). The copies of Isaiah discovered in the Qumran caves prove to be remarkably close to the standard Hebrew Bible, varying slightly in the spelling of some names. They give overwhelming confirmation of the reliability of the Masoretic copies.

During the 1900s more than a hundred New Testament manuscripts are found in Egypt.

Scroll of Isaiah

A Ugaritic Grammar is published in the 1960s. Ugaritic is an ancient language similar to Hebrew and helps scholars understand Hebrew vocabulary and poetry.

1970
New American Bible (NAB) Official version of the Catholic Church. Revised New Testament in 1986.

1971
New American Standard Bible (NASB)
Literal word-for-word translation. Updated in 1995.

1971
The Living Bible
Popular paraphrase.

1976
The Good News Bible (Today's English Version) (TEV) Vernacular English translation.

1978
New International Version (NIV)
Dignified, readable.

1982
New King James Version (NKJV)
Modernization of the KJV using the same manuscripts.

1987
New Century Version (NCV) Puts biblical concepts into natural terms.

1989
Jewish New Testament
English translation using traditional Jewish expressions.

1989
New Revised Standard Version "Gender neutral" revision of the RSV.

AD 1900

Modern Translations

The knowledge from newly discovered manuscripts has led to hundreds of new translations.

1885
The English Revised Version

A British revision of the King James Version.

1901
American Standard Version (ASV)

Revision of the King James Version in American English.

1926
Moffatt Bible

A very popular modern-language version.

1931
Smith-Goodspeed, An American Translation

Modern American English.

1952
The Revised Standard Version (RSV)

A revision of the ASV. New Testament revised 1971.

1958
J.B. Phillips' New Testament in Modern English A paraphrase, originally made for youth.

1965
The Amplified Bible

Uses word-for-word ASV with added words to communicate insights on original texts.

1966
Jerusalem Bible

Translation by Catholic scholars in Jerusalem. The New Jerusalem Bible, 1985.

1970
New English Bible

"Timeless" modern English. Revised in 1989.

AD 2000

1991
Contemporary English Version

"Natural, uncomplicated" English.

1995
God's Word

Contemporary English.

1996
New Living Translation (NLT)

A revision of The Living Bible to make it a translation.

1996
New International Reader's Version (NIrV)

A simplified version of the NIV with a 3rd- or 4th-grade reading level.

2001
English Standard Version (ESV) Literal update of the RSV.

2002
The Message (MSG)

A paraphrase from the original languages.

2004
Holman Christian Standard Bible (HCSB)

 Balance between word-for-word and thought-for-thought.

2005
Today's New International Version (TNIV) Modernization of the New International Version.

2005
New English Translation (NET)

Available only on the Internet, with extensive translator's notes.

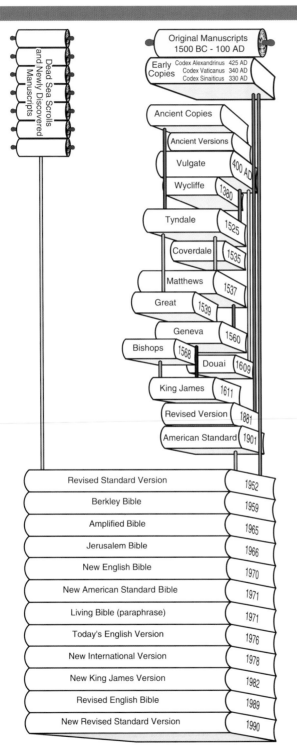

Dead Sea Scrolls and Newly Discovered Manuscripts

Original Manuscripts
1500 BC - 100 AD

Early Copies
Codex Alexandrinus   425 AD
Codex Vaticanus   340 AD
Codex Sinaiticus   330 AD

Ancient Copies

Ancient Versions

Vulgate   400 AD

Wycliffe   1380

Tyndale   1525

Coverdale   1535

Matthews   1537

Great   1539

Geneva   1560

Bishops   1568

Douai   1609

King James   1611

Revised Version   1881

American Standard   1901

Revised Standard Version   1952

Berkley Bible   1959

Amplified Bible   1965

Jerusalem Bible   1966

New English Bible   1970

New American Standard Bible   1971

Living Bible (paraphrase)   1971

Today's English Version   1976

New International Version   1978

New King James Version   1982

Revised English Bible   1989

New Revised Standard Version   1990

Contributors: Philip W. Comfort, Ph.D., Visiting Professor, New Testament (1986-96), Wheaton College, and Senior Editor of Tyndale House Publishers; Errol F. Rhodes, Asst. Dir, Bible Study Helps, American Bible Society; John McRay, Ph.D., Prof. of New Testament and Archaeology, Wheaton College Grad. Sch.; Lawrence Scrivani; Michael Cochrane, M.A., Semitic Languages.
Original Art: Rick Humphrey Photo Credits: Jerome, Wycliffe, Gutenberg Bible page, Northwind Picture Archives; Erasmus, Dead Sea Scrolls, Isaiah Scroll, Erich Lessing; Queen Mary I, Scala; Lindisfarne Gospels, Bridgeman/Art Resources; Scribe, Bibliotique Nacional Paris; Coptic ms., The British Library; William Tyndale, The Principal, Fellows and Scholars of Hartford College, Oxford. Used with permission.

Chart idea and dates courtesy of *Back to the Bible Broadcast*, Lincoln, NE. Used by permission.

The Dead Sea Scrolls

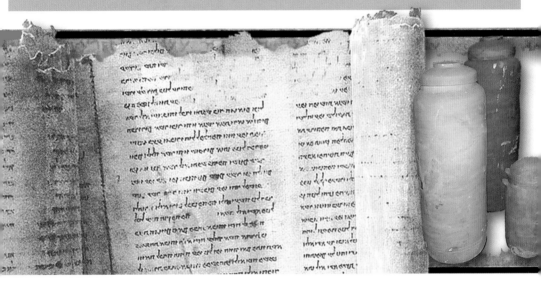

Evidence that Supports the Authenticity of the Bible

New Insights into Life and Culture at the Time of Jesus

How the Scrolls Were Found and Their Importance

WHAT ARE THE DEAD SEA SCROLLS?

The Dead Sea Scrolls are a collection of 931 documents discovered over a half century ago in a region of the Judean desert in what is today called the West Bank. The scrolls date from different periods—as early as 300 BC to AD 40—and were hidden in caves along the edge of the Dead Sea. The discovery of the Dead Sea Scrolls is the greatest literary and archaeological discovery of our time. The scrolls are not the original documents that make up the Hebrew Bible (the Old Testament), but they are the oldest copies of those documents that we have today. The Dead Sea Scrolls have shed new light on the practice of the Jewish religion during the periods when the books of the Bible were composed. They have given us a snapshot of the world Jesus ministered in with his twelve disciples. And they have helped us better understand the society in which the early church first started.

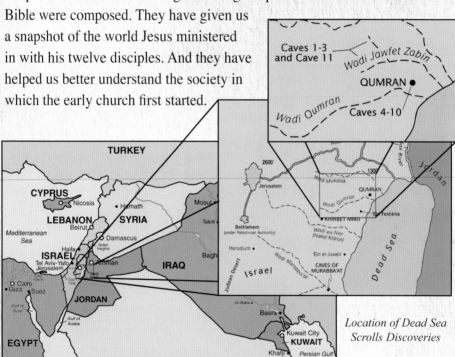

Location of Dead Sea
Scrolls Discoveries

People and
Events in Israel

Beginning of return of ●   Esther becomes queen ●
exiles to Jerusalem

Second Temple is built and dedicated ●
Joshua serves as Zadokite high priest (Haggai 1:1) ●

700 BC	600 BC	500 BC

Events at Qumran   ‖ 25 years between lines

WHAT ARE THE DEAD SEA SCROLLS?

The scrolls are believed to be from the "library" of a group of first-century Jews who separated themselves from the rest of society by living out in the desert at a site known as Qumran. The scrolls contain a variety of writings: portions of every book of the Old Testament except the Book of Esther, commentaries on the books of the Bible, rules for religious rituals and community life, texts designed to prepare the Qumran sect for a war at the End of Time, marriage contracts, deeds of sale, calendars, horoscopes, and writings that claimed to foretell the future.

Canonical Division (According to the Hebrew Bible)	Old Testament Book	Number of Qumran and other Manuscripts (?=possible fragment)
Pentateuch (Torah)	Genesis	24
	Exodus	18
	Leviticus	18
	Numbers	11
	Deuteronomy	33
Prophets (Nevi'im) Former Prophets	Joshua	2
	Judges	3
	1-2 Samuel	4
	1-2 Kings	3
Latter Prophets	Isaiah	22
	Jeremiah	6
	Ezekiel	6
	Twelve (Minor) Prophets	10
Writings (Ketubim)	Psalms	39
	Proverbs	2
	Job	6
The Five Scrolls	Song of Songs	4
	Ruth	4
	Lamentation	4
	Ecclesiates	3
	Esther	0*
	Daniel	8
	Ezra-Nehemiah	1
	1-2 Chronicles	1
	Total	231
	Adjusted	223*

*The total has been adjusted to read 8 less, since 6 scrolls from Qumran contain portions of two books (counted 2X), and 1 scroll from Wadi Murabba'at contains portions of 3 books (counted 3x).

Qumran Manuscripts, which are copies of Books of the Old Testament

The texts are composed in three languages—Hebrew, Aramaic, and Greek. They are written on leather parchment (made from goat or sheep skins) and papyrus (a form of early paper). One scroll is inscribed on pure copper and is known as the Copper Scroll. It appears to be a treasure map, detailing directions to 66 places throughout the Judean desert where immense amounts of gold, silver, and other precious items were hidden. Due to the secretive and mysterious way the texts were written and the loss of identifying physical features in the region today, all attempts to locate the treasure have thus far proven unsuccessful.

Simon II anointed high priest ●
● Nehemiah completes walls of Jerusalem
● Alexander the Great conquers Israel
Ptolemy IV attempts to enter temple ●

400 BC   **300 BC**   **200 BC**

Qumran sect in Damascus? ●

HOW WERE THE SCROLLS DISCOVERED?

In 1946, shepherds of the Ta'amireh Bedouin tribe settled in a desert area between Bethlehem and the Dead Sea, where they tended their flocks and herds. According to local hearsay, a teenager by the name of Muhammed edh-Dhib ("Muhammed the Wolf") went in search of a stray goat. Believing it to have wandered into one of the caves that

Inside Cave 1

honeycombed the limestone cliffs, he threw a rock into the cave to scare it out. Instead of hearing the bleat of a goat, he heard the sound of breaking pottery.

He climbed up into what is today called Cave 1 and found ancient clay storage jars filled with seven scrolls. Four of these scrolls were sold in Bethlehem to an antiquities dealer known as Kando. He in turn sold them for $97.20 to the archbishop of the Monastery of St. Mark's in Jerusalem,

the Metropolitan (a high office in the priesthood of the Syrian Orthodox Church) Mar Athanasius Yeshue Samuel. The other three were sold to Feidi Salahi, another antiquities dealer in Bethlehem, who in turn sold them to Hebrew University Professor Eleazar Sukenik in Jerusalem.

● Simon anointed high priest. Jews rule themselves for 79 years		Alexander Jannaeus in civil war with Pharisees, who are aided by Demetrius III Eucaerus
● Antiochus IV desecrates the temple; the Maccabean Revolt begins	● Jerusalem besieged by Antiochus VII Sidetes of Syria	
● Death of Judas Maccabeus (leader of the revolt)	● John Hyrcanus destroys Samaritan temple on Mt. Gerizim; forces the Judaization of Idumea	
150 BC	**125 BC**	**100 BC**
Period Ia founding of settlement; ● time of John Hyrcanus (?) (late date)	Period Ib begins, marked by building at ● time of Alexander Jannaeus, leader of Judea	
● Founding of Qumran Settlement near the Dead Sea (early date)		

HOW WERE THE SCROLLS DISCOVERED?

The Bedouin shepherds searched more caves, bringing most of their finds to Kando. Meanwhile, the Metropolitan permitted John Trever of the American Schools of Oriental Research to publish news and photographs of the find to the world in April 1948. Soon after, British archaeologists conducted a careful survey of the region and discovered several other caves with scrolls, including those along a terrace at Qumran.

Of these, Cave 4 yielded approximately15,000 fragments representing some 600 manuscripts. These were not found in storage jars but beneath the cave floor, indicating a rapid burial because of impending danger—perhaps the Roman invasion of Jewish territory in ad 68 that led two years later to the complete destruction of Jerusalem. Cave 7 was also unique in that it contained the fragments of 19 texts in Greek—the same language used to write the New Testament.

Cave 4

Forces of Aristobulus II besieged by the Roman general Pompey on Temple Mount. Jewish rule falls to Rome on Yom Kippur.

King Herod, aided by Roman general Sosius, takes Jerusalem from Antigonus

Period of Herod the Great's building

75 BC   50 BC   25 BC

Period Ib ends either with Parthian invasion (40 BC) or earthquake (31 BC)

HOW WERE THE SCROLLS DISCOVERED?

When the Arab-Israeli war broke out in 1948, the Metropolitan took his four scrolls to the United States and offered them for sale in an ad in the Wall Street Journal. Yigael Yadin, an archaeologist and the son of Professor Sukenik, anonymously purchased the scrolls for the State of Israel for $250,000.

Later these four scrolls and three others were put on public display at the Shrine of the Book, a museum built in Jerusalem especially for scrolls. The State of Israel also houses other of the scrolls in a climate-controlled basement of the Rockefeller Museum in Jerusalem. Some scrolls are located in other countries, such as the Copper Scroll in the Citadel Museum in Amman, Jordan.

Shrine of the Book

● Ministry of John the Baptist ● Jewish historian Josephus in Galilee
● Crucifixion of Jesus of Nazareth ● Civil war in Jerusalem, leading
● Conversion of Paul to destruction of site of Qumran
● Birth of Jesus of Nazareth Antonius Felix, procurator

AD 1   AD 50   AD 100

● Period II begins, at the time of Herod the Great's death ● Period II ends, destruction at hands of Roman forces during First Jewish Revolt
Period III, Roman military occupation of Qumran

WHAT DO WE KNOW ABOUT THE SITE OF THE SCROLLS?

Many of the scrolls were found in Caves 4-10 along the terrace known as Qumran, where archaeologists were quick to notice ancient ruins of buildings. Because the caves would have only been accessible via the Qumran plateau, archaeologists began to investigate a connection between the scrolls and the site.

Archaeologist Roland de Vaux supported the connection with his discovery of pottery kilns that were used to fire the scroll jars and with his excavation of a two-story building that contained the remains of writing benches and ink wells. Roland de Vaux (in the 1950s), Yitzhak Magen (in the 1990s), and Randall Price (as recently as 2005) have uncovered deposits of animal bones overlaid with sherds (broken pottery). The Dead Sea Scrolls speak of ritual meals, and several scholars contend that the animal bone deposits that were found buried in a ritual manner are the remains of these ritual meals.

Qumran Site

WHAT DO WE KNOW ABOUT THE SITE OF THE SCROLLS?

Some scholars believe that the site of Qumran may have been originally the biblical "City of Salt" mentioned in a list of cities in this region in Joshua 15:61-62. Scholars have suggested the following time line for the historical development of the Qumran site.

There appears to have been two main phases, one beginning in the time of the Jewish king Alexander Jannaeus (134-104 BC) and continuing until a destruction

The Red Sea as seen from Qumran

of buildings in the settlement in 31 BC, and a final phase in the late Second Temple period (4-1 BC) until the destruction of the site in AD 68 by the Roman army's response to the First Jewish Revolt of AD 66-73. Thereafter for a short time the site was turned into a Roman garrison.

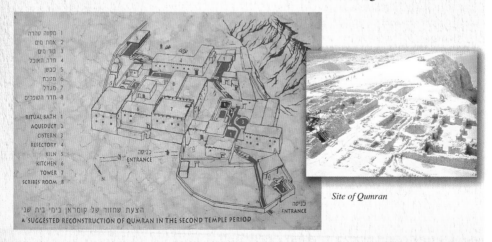

1 מקווה טהרה
2 אמת מים
3 בור מים
4 חדר האוכל
5 כבשן
6 מטבח
7 מגדל
8 חדר הסופרים

RITUAL BATH 1
AQUEDUCT 2
CISTERN 3
REFECTORY 4
KILN 5
KITCHEN 6
TOWER 7
SCRIBES ROOM 8

כניסה ENTRANCE

כניסה ENTRANCE

הצעת שחזור של קומראן בימי בית שני

A SUGGESTED RECONSTRUCTION OF QUMRAN IN THE SECOND TEMPLE PERIOD

Site of Qumran

WHAT DO THE SCROLLS TELL US ABOUT THE OLD TESTAMENT?

T he ancient keepers of the scrolls purposely hid their treasures, trusting that the God of whom they spoke in those documents would guard those documents until the proper time. That time, it turns out, would be our time, some 2,000 years later. Perhaps the most significant single contribution of the scrolls has been their witness to the earliest known text of the Hebrew Bible.

Before the discovery of the scrolls, the oldest known complete Hebrew manuscript of the Old Testament was a Masoretic text (made by Jewish scribes called Masoretes), which is known as the Ben Asher Codex located today in the Public Library of Leningrad, Russia. It dates to about AD 1008. Although this Masoretic version of the Bible is ancient, it was still penned 1,000 years after the last book of the Old Testament was written (around 325 BC). But because it was the oldest existing Hebrew manuscript, the Ben Asher Codex served as basis for the scholarly standard edition of the Hebrew Bible, Kittel's *Biblia Hebraica*, as well as Christian translations of the Old Testament such as the King James Version.

WHAT DO THE SCROLLS TELL US ABOUT THE OLD TESTAMENT?

The Dead Sea Scrolls confirm the accuracy of Bible translation over the years, despite skeptics' accusations that these translations were flawed. As copies of copies of copies of the Old Testament books were made over the centuries, many scholars concluded that mistakes may have been introduced into the Masoretic texts. Comparisons with other ancient versions of the Old Testament, such as the Greek Septuagint, Latin Vulgate, and Samaritan Pentateuch, seemed to confirm this "transmission" problem and called into question the integrity and reliability of the traditional Hebrew text.

These doubts were settled with the discovery in Cave 1 of a copy of the entire Book of Isaiah dated to 125 BC. This is 1,000 years earlier than the Masoretic Ben Asher Codex. When compared to the Ben Asher Codex, this scroll proved to be identical to the later version of Isaiah in more than 95 percent of the text. The 5 percent variation consisted primarily of

Portion of a Scroll

obvious slips of the pen and spelling alterations, many of which are no more significant than the difference in meaning between the word "over" being used in place of the word "above."

This accuracy also proved to be the case for all the other biblical scrolls among the Dead Sea Scrolls. Although interesting differences and additions do appear and are of great value in understanding the history of the transmission of the biblical text, on the whole the witness of the scrolls is to the exceptional preservation of the biblical text through the centuries.

Abbreviations For the Dead Sea Scrolls
Example: 4Q521 2:6
4 = number of the cave in which the document was found
Q = Qumran
521 = designated number for the scroll
2 = column number (abbreviated Col.)
6 = line numbers

This scroll is a reference to Text 521, from Cave 4 at Qumran, column 2, line 6

WHAT DO THE SCROLLS REVEAL ABOUT JEWISH HISTORY?

One thing the scrolls demonstrate is that a number of Jewish groups who separated themselves from society by living in "separatist" communities flourished during what is called the Second Temple Period. The Second Temple Period is the period from 520 BC to AD 70. It is called the "Second Temple" because in 520 BC, the Jews were allowed to rebuild Solomon's temple, which had been destroyed by King Nebuchadnezzar. This second temple stood until it was destroyed by the Romans in AD 70. The separatist

Jewish groups included the Pharisees, Sadducees, the Zealots—all of whom we read about in the Gospel stories—as well as the Essenes, and the Siccari. So far as we know, none of these groups left behind documents concerning their sects. The exception would be the authors and collectors of the Dead Sea Scrolls. Some believe the Essenes produced and collected the scrolls. Whether or not

scrolls belonged to the Essenes, the texts provide historians with original writings on the beliefs and practices of other sects of this period with which the Qumran Jews interacted.

The discovery of the scrolls shows us that Second Temple Judaism, although similar to the older biblical Judaism we read about in the Old Testament, was not identical to it. Neither was Second Temple Judaism identical to what is called Rabbinic Judaism, which began to emerge after the destruction of the Second Temple in AD 70. As a result, the scrolls give us a snapshot of a moment of great disagreement and change in the Jewish practices and beliefs of the day. For example, in many of the writings, the Qumran Jews condemn what they viewed as the ritual abuses of the priests of the day who ran the temple (the same group of Pharisees that Jesus often criticized). Below is a portion of the War Rule. The War Rule is a scroll that contains a prophecy that God would soon destroy these corrupt Temple Jews, as well as a prophecy about the defeat of the Gentile powers oppressing Israel in an end-of-time battle.

The War Rule (Scroll abbreviation: 1QM 1:5-8)
Col. 1⁵[Then the]re* shall be a time of salvation for the People of God, and a time of dominion for all men of His forces, and the eternal annihilation for all the forces of Belial. ⁶There shall be g[reat] panic [among] the sons of Japheth, Assyria shall fall with no one to come to his aid, and the supremacy of the Kittim shall cease, that wickedness be overcome without a remnant. ⁷There shall be no survivors of [all the Sons of] Darkness.

⁸Then [the Sons of Rig]hteousness shall shine to all ends of the world, continuing to shine forth until [the] end of the appointed seasons of darkness.

* [ ] brackets indicate proposed translation or difficult or missing letters or words.

WHAT DO THE SCROLLS REVEAL ABOUT EARLY CHRISTIANITY?

The scrolls opened a window into the time surrounding the climactic events leading up to the birth of the early church, a period that witnessed the development of an end-times movement in Judaism, the birth and ministry of Jesus, the destruction of Jewish independence, the rise of Christianity, and the formation of Rabbinic Judaism.

More particularly, the messianic emphasis (that the long-awaited Messiah of Israel would soon come with power) and prophetic orientation found in many of the scrolls provide insight into the religious viewpoint expressed in the New Testament and early Christianity. When considering the history and religious controversy depicted in the scrolls, it reaffirms the Jewishness of Jesus, the Gospels, and Christianity. In addition the scrolls help us better understand the Apostle Paul's vocabulary and his discussion of customs.

The scrolls also provide help in resolving questions related to Christian interpretation of the Old Testament. For example, Christian tradition has accepted the reading of the Greek Septuagint version of Psalm 22:16, which reads: "They have pierced my hands and feet." This reading appeared to justify a messianic interpretation, where this statement was a prophecy of Christ's crucifixion. At odds with this reading was the Hebrew-language Masoretic Text, which reads "like a lion are my hands and my feet." Because of this it was thought those who made the Septuagint translation (followed here by the New Testament) had mistakenly read the Hebrew word as a verb (= "pierced") rather than a noun (= "lion"). However, the Greek Septuagint, and Christian copyists, were proven to be correct when the Psalms Scroll clearly indicated a verb instead of a noun and reads "they pierced" rather than "like a lion."

Temple Scroll

WHAT DO THE SCROLLS REVEAL ABOUT THE NEW TESTAMENT?

S ince the scrolls generally come to us from a time before the formation of Christianity, they offer a context for understanding the expected nature and role of the Messiah in Judaism. Many of the scrolls from Cave 4 demonstrate a high view of the coming Messiah as being a divine agent with supernatural qualities and powers. These words from a Cave 4 scroll illustrate this understanding:

The Messianic Apocalypse (Scroll abbreviation: 4Q521 2:6-13)

Col. 2⁶His spirit will hover over the humble, and He renews the faithful in His strength. ⁷For He will glorify the pious with the th[ro]ne of His eternal kingdom, ⁸free the captives, open the eyes of the blind, raise up those op[pressed]. ⁹And for[ev]er I shall hold fast [to] the [ho]peful and pious [...] ¹⁰[...] holy [Messiah] will be delayed [...] ¹¹and the Lord shall do glorious things which have not been done, just as He said. Lord.

¹²For He shall heal the critically wounded, He shall resurrect the dead, He shall proclaim good news to the poor, ¹³He shall [...], He shall lead the [ho]ly ones, and the hungry He shall enrich...

The scrolls also explained the sense of prophetic purpose of the Qumran sect in the Judean desert in terms of Isaiah's statement, "A voice is crying, Prepare a way for the Lord in the wilderness" (Isaiah 40:3), the same expression of purpose given by John the Baptist in the Gospels. The scrolls also contain "beatitudes" (4Q525) similar to those of Jesus' Sermon on the Mount (Matthew 5:3-12) and on the Plain (Luke 6:20-23), use vocabulary unique to the New Testament ("sons of light," "works of righteousness," "Belial"), and have similar political and social views on such subjects as predestination, the Temple, divorce, and prophetic events climaxing in a messianic age. With respect to motive for the Sanhedrin's condemnation of Jesus and approval for the Roman punishment of crucifixion, the Temple Scroll shows that the condemnation was based on an interpretation of Deuteronomy 21:22-23 in which the punishment of hanging a man on a tree is mentioned. The Temple Scroll states that this was the prescribed punishment for sedition (betraying the Jewish nation), and this agrees with the statement of the high priest Caiaphas in John 11:49 that Jesus was guilty of this crime.

The discovery of the Dead Sea Scrolls was heard around the world, because the scrolls prove the accuracy of the Bible we have today, shed light on the culture in which Jesus lived, and provide fresh and new insight into the context of early Christianity.

THE HISTORY OF QUMRAN

Period	Date	Main Development of Building Projects
Israelite Period	7th-8th centuries BC	Enclosure wall, round cistern
Period Ia	c. 134-104 BC	Two rectangular cisterns, inlet channel
Period Ib	c. 103-31 BC	Tower, more cisterns, western block, use of south plateau
Interruption in Occupation (31-4 BC) Buildings destroyed by fire, allegedly as the result of an earthquake (reported to have occurred in 31 BC by Joseph Flavius, *War* 1:270-72; *Antiquities* 15:121-22).		
Period II	c. 4 BC-AD 68	Repairs to Ib structures, two reservoirs, use of south plateau
Destruction of Jewish Settlement (AD 68 by Roman Army)		
Period III	after AD 68	Use of part of main block, southeast cistern, water-channel

Author: J. Randall Price, Ph.D, author of *Secrets of the Dead Sea Scrolls and The Stones Cry Out: What Archaeology Reveals about the Truth of the Bible*, is the Director of Excavations at the Qumran Plateau and is president of World of the Bible Ministries, Inc.

50 Proofs
for the Bible
Old Testament

Archeological Finds that Help Confirm the Bible's Accuracy

50 Finds that Help Us Understand the Bible Better

Finds that Help Explain Bible Backgrounds and Cultures

Archaeological Find	Description of the Find	Importance of the Find
1. The Sumerian King List, One of History's First Mentions of a Great Flood The Sumerians established the first civilization in the biblical world. Several clay tablets and prisms containing the list of their kings have been found in the ruins of Mesopotamia.	Surviving copies of the Sumerian king list date to c. 2100 BC. What is striking about the list is that the kings are divided into two groups—those who ruled before a great flood and those who ruled after it. Equally striking is that the lengths of reigns (and life spans) of these kings drastically decreased after the flood, as did life spans of people recorded in the Bible.	The king list says, "After the flood had swept over the earth and when kingship was lowered again from heaven . . ." Mention of a flood, hardly necessary in a list of kings, is an argument for the biblical flood described in Genesis 7-8.
2. An Ancient Flood Story Accounts of a massive flood are found in many cultures around the world. The Gilgamesh Epic (the saga of an ancient Babylonian king, Gilgamesh) includes an expanded flood story on Tablet 11, similar to the flood story in Genesis 6-9. The best known copy of the Epic was found at Nineveh on a series of baked clay tablets.	Tablet 11 of the Gilgamesh Epic tells of a great flood brought on earth by the wrath of gods and includes a hero who is told to build a ship, to take every kind of animal along, and to use birds to check if the water had receded.	Copies of the Epic and other flood stories have been found in the Near East. The popularity of the flood theme argues for its historicity and supports the flood of Noah's time.

Genesis

Genesis

Arvel Witte

Fragment (6 inches high) of a copy of the Babylonian epic of Gilgamesh dating from the 7th century BC, found at Nineveh.

Zev Radovan

Copied piece from the 15th century BC, found in Megiddo, shows the writing.

Genesis
Nehem.

3. Ur, Hometown of Abraham

Ur is mentioned four times in the Bible as the hometown of Abraham. It was occupied from the 4th millennium BC. Excavations of Ur (in Iraq today) have continued off and on since the 1800s.

Carol Witte

The famous Royal Tombs at Ur (c. 2500 BC) reveal gold and silver objects of great beauty.

Part of the "Standard of Ur," from those tombs, made before Abraham, show Sumerian people.

Finds show that Abraham's ancestral home had been a powerful city-state before it fell. If Ur's decline and fall came during Abraham's time, perhaps archaeology has provided another clue as to why Abraham's father relocated his family to Haran. Genesis 11:31; 15:7; Nehemiah 9:7; Acts 7:2-4.

Archaeological Find	Description of the Find	Importance of the Find
Genesis **4. Beni Hasan Tomb Painting** This ancient Egyptian tomb painting, dating close to the time of Abraham, shows a caravan of people from Palestine carrying merchandise for trade in Egypt. They carried eye paint to sell and armed themselves with bows and spears.	 Zev Radovan *Part of the Beni Hasan tomb painting showing Semitic people from Canaan.*	Dating to around 1900 BC, this tomb painting, with words and pictures on it, shows how Old Testament people from the time of Abraham and Sarah looked, how they dressed, their hair styles, and even a musical instrument of the day (lyre). The weapons they used (spear, bow and arrow, ax, sword) depict some of the armaments available to Abraham (Genesis 14).
Exodus Leviticus Deut. **5. The Law Code of Hammurapi** This black diorite stele (a carved upright stone slab) was commissioned around 1750 BC by Hammurapi (Hammurabi), king of Babylon. It contains about 300 laws. The stele was found, partially defaced, at Susa (in Iran today) where it was taken as loot in the 12th century BC.	On top of the Code of Hammurapi, the king is shown in front of a seated deity, Marduk. The king's laws are written on the remainder of the stele for public display. The stele is over seven feet tall.  Zev Radovan	Some of the laws, and the way they are written, are remarkably similar to those found in Exodus, Leviticus, and Deuteronomy, indicating that a "common law" existed in the ancient Near East. For example, *lex talionis* ("an eye for an eye") is found in both the law code of Hammurapi and in Exodus 21:24. Unlike Hammurapi's law, the biblical law is between God and His people.
Genesis **6. Boghazkoy, Hittite Capitol** The ancient Hittites' large capitol city has been discovered about 90 miles east of Ankara, Turkey. The Hittite's rule extended to Syria and Lebanon.  *Warrior god from King's Gate.*	 *Hittite artifacts shown at the Museum of Anatolian Civilizations at Ankara, Turkey.* *Excavations uncovered fortified gateways, temples, and a large archive.*	Although Hittites are mentioned often in the Old Testament, almost nothing was known about them until modern times. One hundred years ago, critics thought the Hittites were an imaginary people made up by the biblical authors. Finding the Hittite's empire forced that claim to be withdrawn and supported the biblical record. The find also helps explain the language, history and literature of people who appear in the Old Testament and ruled in the 2nd millennium BC.

Archaeological Find	Description of the Find	Importance of the Find
7. Nuzi Tablets Excavations at the ancient city of Nuzi east of the Tigris River turned up over 20,000 baked clay tablets.	Dating between 1500-1401 BC, many of these tablets, with cuneiform writing on them, reveal customs and stories very similar to those found in Genesis 15-31, such as marriage, adopting an heir, surrogate mothers, and inheritance.	Because culture changed very slowly in the ancient Near East, the tablets help explain some of the common practices and background which are found in earlier biblical events of the patriarchal period (2000-1500 BC).
8. Haran, Home of the Patriarchs A village of Harran (Haran) exists in Turkey today, and has been found to stand atop the ancient one from the Old Testament period.	Also found near Haran are villages that still bear the names of Abraham's great-grandfather and grandfather, Serug and Nahor, as mentioned in Genesis 11:22-26. Haran was the father of Lot (Genesis 11:27).	The cities of Ur and Haran both had the moon god as their main deity. Terah, father of Abraham, worshiped "other gods" (Joshua 24:2) and moved his family from Ur, in southern Mesopotamia (Iraq today), to Haran in the north (Genesis 11:27-31).
9. Shechem Shechem was strategically placed in the central hill country. It controlled all the roads in the area, but its location made the city vulnerable to attack. Excavations in the city of Shechem reveal a city with walls made of large megalithic stones and the city gate system.	The most important find is a fortress-temple of Baal from the story of Abimelech (Judges 9:46). People could find refuge in the temple from enemies. Before Abimelech, Abraham and Jacob built altars to God in the area of Shechem (Genesis 12, 33) and after the Exodus, the Israelites renewed their covenant with God at Shechem (Joshua 24).	Shechem is important in many biblical stories. It was a city of refuge for anyone who unintentionally caused death (Joshua 20), In the 10th century BC, King Jeroboam I fortified the city and made it the capitol of the kingdom of Israel (1 Kings 12:25). Shechem's vulnerability to attack may be one reason the capitol was moved shortly after Jeroboam I died.

Genesis

Genesis

Genesis
Joshua
Judges
1 Kings

Archaeological Find	Description of the Find	Importance of the Find
Exodus **10. Pithom and Raamses, Store Cities of the Pharaoh** The location of Raamses is now associated with Qantir (Tell el-Dab'a). Pithom was within the Wadi Tumilat, a natural corridor in and out of Egypt, but its exact location is not yet settled.	Ongoing excavations at Tell el-Dab'a (Raamses) have revealed a prosperous ancient city with many monuments, temples, and buildings. Tell el-Retaba is thought to be the most probable location of Pithom, but sufficient excavation has not been done at the site.	According to Exodus 1, the Hebrews were slaves in the Egyptian cities of Pithom and Raamses before the Exodus. The Egyptians forced the Hebrews to make bricks, both with and without straw (Exodus 1:14a; 5:7-19).
Exodus 1 Kings **11. Horned Altars** Excavations have turned up some excellent examples of horned altars.  Zev Radovan	Horned altars made of stone have been found at places like Dan and Beersheba. This reconstructed horned altar (left) dates from the 10th century BC and was found at the city of Beersheba. It was most likely a pagan altar. It was obviously made of dressed (cut) stone, a practice prohibited by the LORD in Exodus 20:25.	The Old Testament speaks of horned incense altars at least 20 times. This find shows how horned altars were shaped. The Bible tells how they were used. One was in the Tabernacle. The LORD told Moses to make an acacia-wood horned altar five cubits long, five cubits broad, and three cubits high with the horns of it at the four corners and overlaid with brass (Exodus 27:2; 1 Kings 1:50).
12. Merneptah (Merenptah) Stele (also called The Israel Stele) The hieroglyphic text of the stele made in Egypt describes the victories of Pharaoh Merneptah around 1230 BC over the Libyans and people of Palestine. The stele stands more than seven feet high. Zev Radovan	The Merneptah Stele contains the earliest extrabiblical mention of the name "Israel" thus far known. The Egyptian pharaoh brags of a victory over Israel around 1230 BC.	Although this battle between Egypt and Israel is not mentioned in the Old Testament, the stele does show that the Israelites were in fact living in the Promised Land at that time, and that their entrance into the land had already taken place by 1230 BC. *Twice the god Amon-Re and Merneptah are depicted in the center, with goddess Mut at left and god Khonsu at right.*

Archaeological Find	Description of the Find	Importance of the Find
13. The Oldest Picture of Israelites In Egypt, on a long wall of the great Karnak Temple, is a recently identified scene of the aftermath of a battle between the Egyptians and Israelites dating to about 1209 BC.	 Lawrence E. Stager *The drawing of the carved scene shows possibly the Israelites vanquished by the armies of Pharaoh Merneptah. Scene 4 of the Karnak Temple relief, Thebes (Luxor).*	Carved about 200 years after the time of Moses and Joshua, this battle scene is by far the earliest picture of Israelites ever discovered. This same event is also told of on the Merneptah Stele. It shows that the Exodus had taken place and the Israelites were living in the Promised Land by 1200 BC.
14. Jericho, Gateway into the Promised Land The earliest ruins at Jericho date to the Stone Age (Neolithic). A tower (right) found in the Jericho ruins dates back before Abraham's time. The tower is made from stones obtained when the surrounding moat was cut. It was connected to a mudbrick wall.	There is debate over whether Joshua's wall of Jericho has been found. Massive erosion has removed much of the remains of that period, and mud bricks could easily erode away over the centuries. Gretchen Goldsmith	The biblical importance of Jericho is underscored by the fact that it is referred to more than 50 times in the Old Testament. Perhaps the most significant references are those in Joshua 6, which tell of the Israelite conquest of the city, their first victory in the Promised Land. Archaeology has shown where the city once stood, and that it guarded the key spot for entering into the Promised Land from the east.
15. The Philistines and the Temple of Rameses III The earliest known record of the Philistines was carved on the wall of an Egyptian temple at Thebes around 1175-1150 BC. *Temple of Rameses III at Thebes (Luxor).* Arvel Witte	At the Temple of Rameses III, the Philistines are both pictured and listed as being one of several groups of "Sea Peoples" invading the coastal plains from Egypt to Palestine. *The Sea Peoples' boat (right side of picture) being defeated by the Egyptians.*  Oriental Institute, University of Chicago	Philistines are mentioned over 200 times in the Old Testament. This temple record shows when the main wave of Philistines tried to invade Egypt. From Samson (Judges 14-16) to David (I Samuel 17), the Israelites battled constantly against the Philistines for control of much of the Promised Land. This record depicts the dress and armor the Philistines might have worn as they interacted with the Israelites.

Joshua

Judges
I Samuel

Archaeological Find	Description of the Find	Importance of the Find
Numb 1 Kings Jeremiah Hosea **16. Canaanite Gods and Goddesses** Between 1929-1939 excavators found hundreds of stories about Canaanite gods and goddesses written on clay tablets among the ruins of the ancient city of Ugarit, in modern Syria.	The Old Testament repeatedly refers to gods and goddesses, like Baal and Ashtaroth (Asherah or Astarte), which were worshiped by the Canaanites living among the Israelites in the Promised Land. The prophets of Israel strongly warned God's people not to worship these false gods in Numbers 25, 1 Kings 11, Jeremiah 23, and Hosea 13. *Asherah* *Zev Radovan*	These finds reveal many details about the Canaanite religion. They help us better understand how prevalent idol worship was in Israelite cities and show the challenge for the children of Israel to worship the one true God. *Astarte Plaque c. 13th-10th century Canaanite period*  *Zev Radovan*
Judges 1 Kings **17. Dan (Laish), Israel's Northernmost City** Excavations show that the large and well-fortified Canaanite city was destroyed around 1150 BC, after which the city was rebuilt, with Israelite artifacts found thereafter.	*The 4000-year-old mud-brick Gate of Dan from the Middle Bronze Age shows gate system construction in the patriarchal period.* The city of Dan was originally a Canaanite stronghold that was conquered by the tribe of Dan (Judges 18). Dan has more artifacts of biblical significance than almost any other city found so far.	According to Judges 20:1, Israel's northern boundary was the city of Dan. The book of Judges tells us that the children of Dan destroyed a Canaanite city by sword and fire and built their own city. They named the city Dan and set up graven images. The High Place where Jeroboam I erected a gold calf has been found in Dan (1 Kings 12:28-31).
1 Kings 2 Kings 2 Chron. Rev. **18. Megiddo (Armageddon), City of War** Finds reveal ruins of a strong prosperous Canaanite city under ruins of a heavily fortified Israelite city with a strong city gate. *The Canaanite bamah (high place) at Megiddo.* *Zev Radovan* 	Megiddo is on a hill beside a wide plain, a strategic location for many battles. Although Joshua defeated the armies of Megiddo's Canaanite king (Joshua 12:21), the Israelites failed to conquer the city then. Not until the time of David or Solomon, did it come under Israelite control. The gate found at Megiddo was like those associated with Solomon's reign.	Solomon made Megiddo a fortress city in the 900s bc (1 Kings 4:12; 9:15). Later, in 609 bc, King Josiah of Judah was killed in a battle against the Egyptians on the plain beside Megiddo (2 Kings 23:29, 2 Chronicles 35:22). Revelation 16:16 refers to Megiddo (called Armageddon) as the place where the army of Christ battles the forces of Satan in the end times.

Archaeological Find	Description of the Find	Importance of the Find
19. Ashkelon, Philistine Seaport Ongoing excavations (right) since 1985 have discovered the large (about 150 acres) and heavily fortified city of Ashkelon. A small bull figurine was found, illustrating pagan worship.	There is evidence that Ashkelon was a major seaport that traded with other Mediterranean nations. *Ashkelon was one of five major cities of the Philistines (Joshua 13:3 and 1 Samuel 6:17).* Zev Radovan 	The Israelites did not conquer Ashkelon (Judges 1:18-19). Nebuchadnezzar destroyed it in 604 BC as predicted by Jeremiah. The prophets Amos, Jeremiah, Zephaniah, and Zechariah all pronounced condemnation upon the city of Ashkelon (Amos 1:6-8, Jeremiah 25:15-20 and 47:5-7, Zephaniah 2:4-7, Zechariah 9:5).
20. Gezer, Gift to King Solomon Archaeologists have excavated the ancient city of Gezer and found clear evidence of Egyptian destruction, as well as a bit of Solomon's defensive walls and the city gate.	Gezer did not become an Israelite city during the conquest and settlement of the Promised Land (Joshua 16:10; Judges 1:29). The Egyptian Pharaoh destroyed the city and its Canaanite inhabitants, then gave it as a wedding gift when Solomon married Pharaoh's daughter (1 Kings 9:15-17).	The wedding gift shows that Egypt was pulling out of Palestine and considered Solomon stronger. Solomon later rebuilt Gezer as an Israelite stronghold. The similarity of Gezer's gateway to those found at Megiddo and Hazor indicates they were all built by Solomon.
21. Shiloh, First Home of the Ark of the Covenant Archaeology at Shiloh has found an Israelite city from Joshua's time and evidence of subsequent destruction by fire.	According to the Old Testament, Shiloh was an important early sanctuary in the Promised Land. The Tent of Meeting (part of the Tabernacle) and the Ark of the Covenant resided at Shiloh after Joshua's conquest (Joshua 18 and 1 Samuel 1-4).	1 Samuel 4 tells of Israel moving the ark from Shiloh to a battlefield, hoping it would protect them from the Philistines. The Philistines captured the ark in battle. Archaeological evidence indicates that sometime later the Philistines destroyed Shiloh.

Joshua
Judges
1 Samuel
Jeremiah
Amos
Zeph.
Zech.

Joshua
Judges
1 Kings

Joshua
1 Samuel
2 Samuel

Archaeological Find	Description of the Find	Importance of the Find
22. Ashdod, Where Dagon Fell Ashdod was one of the five major Philistine cities mentioned in Joshua 13:3 and 1 Samuel 6:17. Archaeological work between 1962-1969 has yielded much new information about Ashdod. No temple of Dagon has been found, but an open area where there had once been a temple has surfaced.	*"Deity in a Fish-Robe"* was often identified as the Philistine god Dagon, 9th century  BC, found in Assyria in the 1800s. The true appearance of Dagon is uncertain. *Anvil Witte* Archaeologists have found that the Philistine culture had begun to fade away in the city during the 700s BC as Amos prophesied.	In 1 Samuel 5 the Philistines brought the Ark of the Covenant to Ashdod after they captured it in battle. After placing the Ark in the temple of Dagon (the chief Philistine god), the statue of Dagon fell and broke into pieces and the people of the city became infested with tumors. They eventually sent the Ark back to Israel. Some three centuries later the prophet Amos received this word from the LORD, "I will cut off the inhabitants from Ashdod . . . and the remnant of the Philistines shall perish . . ." (Amos 1:8).
23. Shishak's Invasion Record A record of Pharaoh Shishak's raid of 140 places, including the kingdom of Judah has been found in Egypt carved on a wall in the Karnak Temple of Amun, god of Thebes (Luxor today). The Shishak Relief (Sheshonk I) commemorates his victory over Rehoboam when Solomon's temple was robbed of its riches (probably 925 BC). The relief shows that Egypt raided Israel, not just Judah.	 *Karnak Temple* *Above: Egyptian goddess Mut holds a club and bow, and leads five rows of captives.* *Right: Shishak grasps a group of captives by the hair and strikes them with his club.* *Carol Witte*	According to the Old Testament (1 Kings 14 and 2 Chronicles 12), Pharaoh Shishak of Egypt invaded Judah during the fifth year of King Rehoboam's reign. "... Shishak, king of Egypt, came up against Jerusalem, because they had transgressed against the LORD, with twelve hundred chariots, and threescore thousand horsemen; and the people were without number that came with him out of Egypt..." (2 Chronicles 12:2-3). Other verses that refer to Thebes (the city of No) in Egypt are Jeremiah 46:25 and Ezekiel 30:14-16.
24. Beth Shemesh Excavations now underway at the ancient fortified city of Beth Shemesh have already yielded both Philistine and Israelite artifacts, as well as evidence of its destruction as described in 2 Chronicles 12. *Zev Radovan* 		According to 1 Samuel 6:12-15, the Philistines returned the captured Ark of the Covenant to the Israelites at Beth Shemesh. Later, about 940 BC, Pharaoh Shishak of Egypt invaded and destroyed several cities in the foothills region (2 Chronicles 12:2-4). Also, discoveries of massive fortifications and a water supply show Solomon's building activity in the city.

Joshua
1 Samuel
2 Samuel
Amos

1 Kings
2 Chron.
Jeremiah
Ezekiel

1 Samuel
2 Chron.

Archaeological Find	Description of the Find	Importance of the Find
25. Pool at Gibeon This remarkable pool, dating to before 1000 BC, was found largely intact in Gibeon, six miles north of Jerusalem in excavations around in 1956.	The Pool of Gibeon goes down some 80 feet. The original diggers removed 3000 tons of limestone. A tunnel for the pool runs under the city to an outside spring. This internal water supply was important in case of siege.	2 Samuel 2:13 and Jeremiah 41:12 speak of a great water pool at Gibeon. The find verifies the location of the Pool at Gibeon as mentioned in the Bible and shows the great effort taken to have a secure source of water.
26. Gibeah, King Saul's Capitol Archaeologists have identified Gibeah with the ancient ruins on a hill known today as Tel el-Ful, about three miles north of Jerusalem.	Excavations have shown that the site of Gibeah was inhabited about 1100 BC, the time of King Saul. Saul's fortress-palace was found here. It was small and modest compared with the later palaces of David and Solomon.	Gibeah was the principal town of the tribe of Benjamin (Judges 19:11-14). It was also Saul's home. He eventually made it his capitol (1 Samuel 10:26; 11:4; and 15:34). Finding Gibeah so close to Jebusite Jerusalem indicates that Saul never fully controlled the land.
27. Beth Shean Archaeology shows that Canaanites, and possibly Philistines, occupied Beth Shean from the time of the Judges until after Saul. Beth Shean was a city within the tribal allotment of Manasseh (Joshua 17:11). However, the Israelites did not conquer Beth Shean (Judges 1:27), and the Philistines eventually took it.	 *Gretchen Goldsmith* *Beth Shean is the large tell in the background.* Later King Saul and his armies fought the Philistines on Mt. Gilboa. King Saul and his sons (all but one) died in the battle.	The Philistines hung the bodies of King Saul and his sons from the walls of Beth Shean (1 Sam. 31:10). See the large tell (hill) at left. Some believe that finding Philistine coffins shows that the Philistines occupied the city at or before the time of Saul. *Philistine coffin lid from nearby cemetery.*  Arvel Witte

2 Samuel
Jeremiah

Judges
1 Samuel

Joshua
Judges
1 Samuel

Archaeological Find	Description of the Find	Importance of the Find
28. King David's Jerusalem The City of David Archaeological Project uncovered much of the buried remains of David's city of Jerusalem between 1978-1985.	Archaeologists have uncovered remains of that city, including evidence of David's conquest and a palace that may have belonged to King David himself. The most important find has been that the Siloam spring was guarded by towers.	According to the Old Testament books of 2 Samuel and 1 Chronicles, King David conquered Jerusalem and made it the capitol of Israel. Virtually nothing apart from the Bible was known about the city of that time until excavations were done between 1978-85.
29. The House of David Inscription (Dan Inscription) In 1993 and 1994 an archaeologist working at the Old Testament site of the city of Dan found three pieces of an inscribed stone referring to David. *House of David inscription on black basalt stone (detailed)*  *Zev Radovan*	This stone inscribed in Aramaic with the expression "the house of David", refers to King David's descendants. Originally part of a victory pillar of a neighboring king of Damascus (possibly Hazael), the stone has been dated to two or three centuries after David's time. It mentions a "king of Israel," possibly Joram son of Ahab, and a king of the "House of David," possibly Ahaziah of Judah.	This Tel Dan inscription is a very important find because it is the first reference to King David found outside of the Bible.  *Zev Radovan* *House of David inscription on black basalt stone.*
30. Beersheba, Southern Boundary of the Promised Land Excavations between 1969-1976 uncovered the Israelite city of Beersheba with its strong defensive walls and a massive city gate, built after David's time.	Beersheba was found to have a large well, long storehouses, and private residences which date to the 1st millennium BC. *Zev Radovan* 	Beersheba eventually became Israel's key fortress city in the south during the period of King Solomon (1 Kings 4:25). Finding the strong walls and gate supports the Bible account of Beersheba after the time of David.

2 Samuel / 2 Chron.
2 Kings
Judges / 1 Kings

Archaeological Find	Description of the Find	Importance of the Find
31. Samaria, Capitol of the Northern Kingdom of Israel *1 Kings, 2 Kings, 2 Chron., Hosea, Amos, Micah* Few cities are mentioned more times in the Old Testament than Samaria. Excavations have uncovered much of the city and have found it to have been extravagant, prosperous, and strong.	For most of the history of the kingdom of Israel—after the kingdom was split in two following Solomon's rule—Samaria was the third, and last, capitol of the Northern Kingdom. The Bible speaks of this well-fortified city built by King Omri and King Ahab. *Samarian ivory furniture inlay, 8th cent. BC*  *Arvel Witte*	Although much of the ruins of the Old Testament period were destroyed when King Herod built over and through earlier levels, enough has been found to show that Samaria was extravagant and strong, as described in the Old Testament. See 1 Kings 16:24, 2 Kings 6-22, 2 Chronicles 18, and the prophets Hosea, Amos, and Micah. Amos refers to houses and beds of ivory (Amos 3:15; 6:4).
32. Hazor, Key to Israelite Victory *Joshua, 1 Kings* Archaeology has found evidence of fiery destruction of Hazor, the major city of the north during the Conquest, possibly by the forces of Joshua (Joshua 11).	The rebuilding and fortification by Solomon parallels what he did at Megiddo and Hazor. The distinctive gates were found to be nearly identical to gates of these cities.	Finding that Hazor occupied about 200 acres, far larger than a normal city in that day, provides reason for the Bible calling it "the head." The city's king, Jabin, rallied the kingdoms in the north against the Israelites. Yet the forces of Joshua prevailed (Joshua 11).
33. Ivory Ornaments and Objects *1 Kings, 2 Chron.* Decorative ivory has been found in several sites in Palestine, including Megiddo and Samaria. *Zev Radovan*	Below is an ivory pomegranate, found in a dealer's shop, possibly an ornament (thought to have been atop a scepter) from Solomon's temple. The inscription says: "Belonging to . . . Holy to the Priest."	According to 1 Kings 10:18 and 2 Chronicles 9:17, King Solomon had a throne made of ivory covered with gold. "The king made a great throne of ivory, and overlaid it with the best gold" (1 Kings 10:18). The authenticity of the inscription is disputed.

Archaeological Find	Description of the Find	Importance of the Find
34. The Gezer Calendar This small palm-sized limestone tablet bears one of the first known examples of Hebrew writing (971-913 BC).	Found at Gezer, one of King Solomon's fortress cities, this tablet contains a school memorization drill—a short poem about the agricultural seasons in biblical Palestine.	The text gives insight into when certain tasks were done during the agricultural year. It shows literacy in the 10th century BC.
35. House of Yahweh Ostracon This find appears to be a receipt for a donation of three shekels of silver to the House of Yahweh (Solomon's Temple).	This ostracon (writing on a piece of pottery) is 4 inches wide and 3½ inches tall. It is not known where it was found. Some scholars date it between 835 and 796 BC, some 130 years after the Temple was built.	This extremely important find is the oldest mention of Solomon's Temple that has been found outside the Bible. *House of YHWH ostracon* *Shlomo Moussaleff*
36. Seals from the Royal Courts of Israel and Judah Excavations at several sites in modern Israel and antiquity shops have turned up carved semi-precious stones belonging to members of the royal courts of kings in the Old Testament.	Dating from about 900 BC to about 600 BC, these stones were used to press images into pieces of clay that sealed up kings' important documents. One of the most famous seals, found at Megiddo, depicts a lion with the words, "belonging to Shema, servant of Jeroboam." Seals with the names of other kings were found also (See 1 and 2 Kings).	Seals were found for Uzziah (around 760 BC), Hoshea (around 730 BC), and Hezekiah (around 700 BC). The seal at the right says "SHLOMO" (Solomon) in Hebrew. *Zev Radovan*

Genesis Exodus Numb. Joshua 1 Kings 2 Kings Psalms Isaiah

1 Kings 2 Chron.

1 Kings 2 Kings 2 Chron.

Archaeological Find	Description of the Find	Importance of the Find
37. The Moabite Stone In 1868, a German missionary found a stone slab over three feet tall near Dibon, east of the Dead Sea. Inscribed on the stone were the accomplishments of Mesha, king of Moab around 850 BC. This stone is sometimes called the Mesha Stele. *Genesis 2 Kings*	The ancient Moabites were relatives of the Israelites according to Genesis 19:37. On this stone King Mesha brags of having driven the Israelites out of his land. 2 Kings 3 tells that the king of Moab rebelled against the king of Israel after the death of King Ahab of Israel.	The Moabite stone is one of the earliest finds that mention biblical people. The stone says that King Omri and his son Ahab "humbled" Moab for many years. After Ahab's death, King Mesha said he had "triumphed" over Ahab's family and that Israel had "perished forever." Some scholars say that the stone also contains a reference to the "house of David." *Zev Radovan*
38. The Black Obelisk of Shalmaneser This 6½ foot tall black basalt obelisk (four-sided pillar) reports in pictures and words the conquests of Assyrian King Shalmaneser III, enemy of the Israelites.  *Arvel Witte* *2 Kings*	The Black Obelisk was discovered in the palace at Nimrud in 1846 and shows the biblical Jehu, king of Israel, kneeling down and bringing tribute to the Assyrian king, Shalmaneser. Dating from 841 BC, this important find is the only picture we have so far of an Israelite king. This is the first mention of tribute paid to Assyria by Israel. King Jehu's reign is mentioned in 2 Kings 9-10, even though the tribute is not.	 *Arvel Witte* *Part of the inscription reads: "Tribute of Jehu the Israelite."*
39. King Uzziah's Burial Plaque A stone plaque, found on the grounds of the Russian church on the Mt. of Olives, reads: "Here, the bones of Uzziah, King of Judah, were brought. Do not open." *2 Chron.*	King Uzziah ruled Judah 792-740 BC, at the time that Amos, Hosea and Isaiah were prophesying. He was 16 years old when he became king and he reigned in Jerusalem for 52 years. As long as he sought the LORD, God gave him success.	According to 2 Chronicles 26, Uzziah sinned against the LORD and was stricken with a leprous disease toward the end of his life, and upon his death was buried in a "field of burial that belonged to the kings."

Archaeological Find	Description of the Find	Importance of the Find
40. The Siloam Tunnel Inscription *2 Kings* *2 Chron.* Two boys discovered this ancient Hebrew inscription carved in stone along the wall of a tunnel as they were wading through the southern end of the tunnel's waters in 1880.	The inscription comes from the days of King Hezekiah (701 BC) who ordered the tunnel to be made so the water from Jerusalem's Gihon Spring could be brought into the city to a man-made reservoir, the Pool of Siloam. This tunnel provided water to Jerusalem during the anticipated siege of King Sennacherib of Assyria.	The inscription celebrates the completion of this remarkable tunnel as mentioned in 2 Kings 20:20 and 2 Chronicles 32:30. *Siloam Tunnel Inscription found in Hezekiah's Tunnel.*  *Zev Radovan*
41. The Lachish Reliefs *2 Kings* *2 Chron.* Among the ruins of the Nineveh palace of Assyrian King Sennacherib were found 62-foot-long reliefs that picture the fall of the Judean fortress of Lachish in 701 BC, over 100 years before the attack on and fall of Judah.	 *Arvel Witte* *Assyrian troops are shown advancing with stone slingers and archers. Siege towers were wheeled up ramps to batter the city wall.*	These Nineveh palace carvings of the Lachish defeat amplify the biblical record concerning the siege of the kingdom of Judah in the days of King Hezekiah. In 2 Kings 18:13 it says, "Now in the fourteenth year of King Hezekiah did Sennacherib, king of Assyria, come up against all the fenced cities of Judah, and took them." However, before the Assyrians could capture Jerusalem, they were destroyed by "God's angel" and Sennacherib withdrew (2 Kings 20:35; 2 Chronicles 32).
42. Sennacherib Prism *2 Kings* *2 Chron.* *Isaiah* A 15-inch tall, six-sided baked clay prism from ancient Assyria contains the story of the invasion of the kingdom of Judah by Sennacherib in 701 BC. The prism was found at Nineveh.	King Sennacherib of Assyria is mentioned in 2 Kings 18-19. Isaiah prophesied that God would protect Jerusalem against attack by Sennacherib (Isaiah 36-37, 2 Chronicles 32). While the prism does say that the Assyrians trapped Hezekiah in Jerusalem "like a bird in a cage," like the biblical record, it says nothing of them conquering the city.	The Bible says that God spared Jerusalem. The prism, together with the Lachish reliefs and excavations, adds detail to the biblical account. King Hezekiah prayed to the LORD. Isaiah brought him God's message. That night the LORD smote 185,000 Assyrians, and Sennacherib went back to Nineveh and later was killed by his sons (Isaiah 37:35-38).

Archaeological Find	Description of the Find	Importance of the Find
43. The Tomb of the Priestly Hezir Family In an elaborate tomb complex cut into the wall of Jerusalem's Kidron Valley is a Hebrew inscription identifying the burial cave as belonging to the descendants of Hezir.	The names of three generations of priestly Hezir family members also appear in the inscription, verifying the existence of this priestly family mentioned in 1 Chronicles 24:15 and Nehemiah 10:20. 	A list of the Levitical priests during King David's time found in 1 Chronicles 24 includes the name of Hezir. Later, in Nehemiah 10, another priest named Hezir (possibly a descendant of the former Hezir) is listed as one of the priests who signed a covenant to keep God's Law in the restored Temple around 450 BC.
44. Carchemish, Where History Changed Course This city is mentioned only three times in the Bible, but archaeology reveals that it was in a strategic location, desired by the Hittites, Assyrians, and Babylonians.	Carchemish was important in biblical history for one key battle. In 605 BC, the Babylonians defeated the Assyrian and Egyptian armies there. This destroyed the Assyrians and paved the way for the Babylonians to conquer much of the biblical world, including the kingdom of Judah.	In 586 BC, the Babylonians stormed Jerusalem and destroyed the Temple. Jeremiah 46 and 2 Chronicles 35-36 speak of the prophecies and circumstances leading up to the Battle of Carchemish, and the devastating chain of events that followed.
45. The Lachish Letters In 1935 an archaeologist unearthed several letters, written about 588 BC, on 21 pottery pieces (ostraca) from among the burned ruins of the ancient city of Lachish of Judah.	The Lachish messages were desperate pleas by the Judean defenders of the city for military assistance. Apparently the city was conquered by Nebuchadnezzar before the letters could be sent. 	The letters show Judah was trying to obtain help from Egypt, relying on man rather than God. One ostracon mentions that no fire signals from another defensive city, Azekah, could be seen. Jeremiah 34:2-7 prophesied the conquest of Judah, destruction of Jerusalem, and exile to Babylon. See 2 Kings 24-25.

1 Chron.
Nehem.

2 Chron.
Jeremiah

2 Kings
Jeremiah

Arvel Witte

Archaeological Find	Description of the Find	Importance of the Find
Numb. 2 Chron. **46. Silver Amulets** In 1979, while excavating 6th century bc tombs in Jerusalem, excavators found two small amulets (under two inches long) that looked like necklaces made of silver sheets rolled up like miniature scrolls. They date to about Jehoakim's reign in Judah (2 Chronicles 36).	When unrolled, each of the scrolls was found to have the prayer from Numbers 6:24-26 scratched on it: "The LORD bless thee and keep thee; The LORD make his face shine upon thee, and be gracious unto thee: The LORD lift up his countenance upon thee, and give thee peace." This is the first time God's divine name has been found on an artifact from Jerusalem. 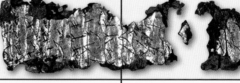	Dating to about 600 BC, these amulets contain the oldest examples of a Scripture passage yet found.
Genesis Isaiah Jeremiah Daniel **47. Babylon** The ruins of ancient Babylon, capitol of the Babylonian Kingdom, cover 2000-3000 acres in Iraq, 56 miles south of Baghdad.	Babylon's ruins include one of many ziggurats (stepped towers) from the area. Later finds include ruins of the palace of King Nebuchadnezzar (Daniel 4:29).  *Ruins of Babylon*	The palace of King Nebuchadnezzar, who destroyed Jerusalem in 586 BC and sent the Jews into exile, was the site of Belshazzar's feast in Daniel 5. Jeremiah wrote that the LORD would make Babylon desolate forever (Jeremiah 25:12; 51). The present ruins also echo the prophecy of Isaiah 13:19-20.
2 Chron. Ezra Isaiah **48. The Cyrus Cylinder** A 9-inch long clay cylinder found at ancient Babylon, dating to 539 BC, tells of King Cyrus of Persia's conquest of Babylon and of his decree to let captives held by Babylon return to their lands and restore their temples.	King Cyrus of Persia (Iran area today) also made a similar decree that the Jews, carried away captive to Babylon, could return to Jerusalem. *Cyrus Cylinder*  *Arvel Witte*	Cyrus sent the Jews back to their homeland after many years of exile in Babylon as Isaiah prophesied (2 Chronicles 36:23; Ezra 1; Isaiah 44:28). This "return-home" decree was one of many issued by Cyrus. Though not mentioning Judah, it confirms that this was Cyrus's policy and gives credibility to the biblical record.

Esther
Daniel

Archaeological Find	Description of the Find	Importance of the Find
49. Susa, Royal City of Queen Esther Located in modern Iran, Susa's ruins have been excavated by several teams during the last century. The most impressive find has been the remains of the elegant royal palace built mainly by Darius (522-486 BC). The book of Esther is set in Susa later. *Right: Frieze of life-size Persian royal guard from the palace of Darius the Great (father of Xerxes I) at Susa.*	Susa ("Shushan" in Hebrew) was one of three royal cities during the reign of King Cyrus of Persia. Xerxes and Artaxerxes carried on the building of the palace complex. A large number of beautiful artifacts and elaborate stone columns were found at Susa. Daniel saw a vision in Susa (Daniel 8:2, c. 551 BC). *Arvel Witte*	Queen Esther (c. 478 BC) was married to King Ahasuerus (Xerxes I) and saved the Jews. Artaxerxes sent Ezra and Nehemiah to rebuild Jerusalem (Ezra 7:14-21; Nehemiah 13:5-8).  *Inscribed silver bowl of Artaxerxes I (c.464-424 BC), son of King Xerxes.* *Arvel Witte*
50. The Dead Sea Scrolls The Dead Sea Scrolls are actually hundreds of scrolls and scraps that date between 300 BC and AD 70. The first of them was found in 1947 in caves in the Qumran area near the Dead Sea about seven miles south of Jericho.	Some of the scrolls were found in jars. About one-third of the scrolls contain copies of portions of Old Testament books (every book but Esther). These copies are over 1000 years older than most of the manuscripts scholars previously had available for study and translation.	This is one of the most important finds in history because it shows that the Old Testament was copied very accurately over the centuries. When the scrolls were compared with the oldest Masoretic text, on which most modern translations are based, only insignificant differences were found. Therefore we can be confident that our current translations are faithful to the original. *Arvel Witte*

Contributors: Professor Larry McKinney, Central Baptist Theological Seminary (Kansas); Dan Master, Assistant Professor of Archaeology, Wheaton College (Illinois); Dr. John Monson, Assistant Professor of Archaeology, Wheaton College (Illinois).

Arrangement of Events
The contents of this chart are generally arranged from the earliest events mentioned in the Bible to the most recent events.

Dates of Events (examples)
1st century BC = 100 BC to 1 BC
2nd century BC = 200 BC TO 101 BC
10th century BC = 1000 BC to 901 BC
13th century BC = 1300 BC TO 1201 BC
1st millennium BC = 1000 BC to 1 BC
2nd millennium BC = 2000 BC to 1001 BC

50 Proofs
for the Bible
New Testament

Archeological Finds that Help Confirm the Bible's Accuracy

50 Finds that Help Us Understand the Bible Better

Finds that Help Explain Bible Backgrounds and Cultures

Archaeological Find	Description of the Find	Importance of the Find

The Life and Ministry of Jesus

Matt
Mark
Luke
John

1. The Church of the Nativity in Bethlehem

Archaeology has shown that the use of caves as animal stables in the Holy Land has been a common practice from very ancient times. Ancient records show that for at least two centuries before a church was built, Christians had marked this particular cave as the place of Jesus' birth.

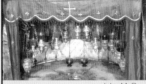

John McRay

Since AD 326 a building known as the Church of the Nativity has stood over a cave at what was the ancient outskirts of Bethlehem.

Matthew 2:1-8, Luke 2:4-15, and John 7:42 all identify Bethlehem as the place of Jesus' birth. Because Joseph and Mary could find no room at the village inn and the newborn Jesus was laid in a manger (animal feedbox), it has been assumed that the birth took place in a stable. The niche at left marks the place that Christians throughout history identified as Jesus' birthplace. Archaeology and tradition combine in this instance to lend both accuracy and insight to the Gospel accounts.

2. Nazareth, Hometown of Jesus

Today Nazareth is a bustling Arab-Jewish city built atop and around the ancient village, located in the southern hills of lower Galilee.

Gretchen Goldsmith

Church of the Annunciation

The modern Church of the Annunciation (left) stands over an ancient church building. Excavations in the church and around its grounds have turned up silos, olive oil presses, foundations of houses, and many artifacts from Christ's time. The nearby Church of St. Gabriel stands over the city's ancient well, and the well is still fed by fresh spring water.

Little would be known about the town where Mary received the angelic news that she would give birth to Christ, and where Jesus grew up, if it were not for the Christian holy places and archaeology. Matthew 2:23, 4:13, Mark 1:9, and Luke 1:26-28 give the New Testament accounts of the events connected with Nazareth. John 1:46 also mentions Nazareth.

3. Bethsaida, City of Woe

Much of the ancient harbor city of Bethsaida has been recovered since 1987 after several seasons of archaeological work. It has finally been placed accurately on biblical maps as a result.

John McRay

Bethsaida was the birthplace of Peter, Andrew, and Philip, and is mentioned in the Gospels more than any other city except Capernaum and Jerusalem. Jesus pronounced a "woe" (condemnation) upon the city in Matthew 11:21 and Luke 10:13. It was destroyed around ad 66-68, and was never rebuilt. Mark 8:22 and John 1:44 also mention Bethsaida.

Archaeological Find	Description of the Find	Importance of the Find
The Life and Ministry of Jesus		

John

4. Cana, Site of a Wedding Feast
Archaeological investigations show that the ruins at Khirbet Qana were a village during the time of Christ. Its ruins are located about nine miles north of Nazareth.

The Gospel of John (John 2:1-11) records the miracle of Jesus turning water into wine during a wedding celebration in the village of Cana.

Cana ruins at Khirbet Qana date to the time of Christ

John McRay

Matt. Mark Luke

5. The House Church at Capernaum

While excavating an early church building at Capernaum in 1968, archaeologists found that the building had been placed over a house from the time of Jesus.

Words were found scratched on the walls of the house indicating that the early Christians believed the house had been that of the apostle Simon Peter.

Matthew 8:14, Mark 1:29, and Luke 4:38 all speak of Peter's house and Jesus' visits there. This may be the reason Christians began to worship at this site.

Matt. Mark Luke John

6. The Synagogue at Capernaum

Archaeologists have restored a synagogue that stood there some 350 years after Jesus' time. However, recently it was discovered that this synagogue was built over the foundation of the synagogue from Jesus' time, confirming that this is the place where important Bible events took place.

Gretchen Goldsmith

A newer synagogue at Capernaum was built on the foundation of the black basalt synagogue of Jesus' time (shown at right).

Capernaum served as Jesus' headquarters during his ministry in Galilee. According to Mark 1:21-28, 3:1-6, Luke 4:31-37, and John 6:59, Jesus both taught and healed people in the synagogue there.

Gretchen Goldsmith

Archaeological Find	Description of the Find	Importance of the Find
The Life and Ministry of Jesus		

Matt
Mark
Luke

7. Gergesa, Where Christ Cast Out Demons

The location of Gergesa has remained a mystery until recently. In 1970 Israeli archaeologist Vasilios Tzaferis investigated ruins of a Byzantine church from ad 585 uncovered during road construction along the east side of the Sea of Galilee.

The excavations turned up an ancient church building, monastery, and chapels. A mosaic-paved chapel had been built at the foot of a steep slope, leading Dr. Tzaferis to conclude that the ancient Christians had built the entire complex here to preserve an early tradition that this was where the miracle occurred in which swine ran off a cliff into the sea.

In Matthew 8:28-34 Christ casts demons out of two men into a herd of swine that ran down a steep place into the Sea of Galilee. Two other possible locations were thought to be Gadara or Gerasa (Mark 5:1-13; Luke 8:26-39) but both are located far from the Sea of Galilee or any steep place. The ruins of the El-Kursi monastery probably mark the location of Gergesa.

John

8. Jacob's Well Near Sychar

The well can be found today beside what archaeologists have identified as the ancient north-south road near Mount Gerizim, in the eastern part of Nablus.

Today the well is still fed by an underground stream, and an unfinished church building covers it.

John 4:1-42 tells the story of Jesus' encounter with a Samaritan woman at Jacob's well. Since ancient times Christian pilgrims have come to the well and have written about it.

Matt
Mark
Luke

9. Jericho, Where Jesus Met Zacchaeus

Most of the ruins of Herod the Great's winter palace at Jericho reveal that it was built in the finest Roman style. Jericho is where Herod the Great built many grand buildings at great public expense.

The Jericho of Jesus' day lay a few miles south of the Old Testament city. Jericho was connected to Jerusalem by means of a 17-mile-long road that ran through a steep valley. Among the structures discovered there were Herod the Great's winter palace and a hippodrome (stadium for horse races and other spectacles).

Herod the Great was king when Jesus was born (Matthew 2:1-12). Jericho was the city where Jesus encountered Zacchaeus, a tax collector (Luke 19:2-10). Jericho is also the setting of Jesus' story of "The Good Samaritan" (Luke 10:30-37).

Archaeological Find	Description of the Find	Importance of the Find
The Life and Ministry of Jesus		
John **10. The Pool of Bethesda in Jerusalem** Site of Jesus' healing of a paralyzed man (John 5:2-11), much of the remains of this pool have been unearthed since 1956.	At right are the ruins of what was the Pool of Bethesda. Portions of the five porticos (roofs supported by columns) mentioned in the Gospel story have been found and can be seen by visitors today.	 *Gretchen Goldsmith* John 5:2 says, "Now there is in Jerusalem near the Sheep Gate a pool, which in Aramaic is called Bethesda and which is surrounded by five covered colonnades."
Matt Mark Luke John **11. Bethany, Where Jesus Raised Lazarus** A village grew around the first-century ad tombs that once comprised Bethany's cemetery. Since early Christian times, one tomb has been said to be that of Lazarus.	By the ad 300s a church had been built over the tomb of Lazarus, with steps leading down into the tomb. Today visitors can still visit that ancient tomb and reflect on the great miracle Jesus performed there.	The village of Bethany is mentioned 13 times in the New Testament. Located on the east side of the Mount of Olives, only a short distance from Jerusalem, it was a favorite stopover for Jesus and the disciples when they came to Jerusalem. It was from Bethany's cemetery that Jesus raised Lazarus (John 11).
12. The Pontius Pilate Inscription In 1961 archaeologists working at the ruins of Caesarea Maritima, in Israel, found a stone slab bearing the name of Pontius Pilate, who was involved in the trial of Jesus.	 *Gretchen Goldsmith* *Portion of the stone bearing Pilate's name, which commemorated his dedication of a temple to Emperor Tiberius.*	This is the oldest appearance of Pilate's name to be found, and it dates to the time of Jesus. Luke 3:1 says: "Now in the fifteenth year of the reign of Tiberias Caesar, Pontius Pilate being governor of Judea, and Herod being tetrarch of Galilee..."

Archaeological Find	Description of the Find	Importance of the Find
The Life and Ministry of Jesus		

The Life and Ministry of Jesus

Matt Mark Luke

13. Caiaphas's Family Tomb

In 1990 builders accidentally uncovered a first- century ad burial cave south of Jerusalem. Later, archaeologists investigated and found several stone boxes (called ossuaries) that contained human bones.

Zev Radovan

The ossuary of Caiaphas, the priest who brought Jesus to trial. Ossuaries were used to store the bones of several generations of family members.

Inside the stone boxes were the bones of two infants, a child, a teenager, a woman, and a man. One box had the name "Caiaphas" on it. The man's bones may be those of Caiaphas, the priest who brought Jesus to trial, mentioned in Matthew 26:57 and John 18:13-14.

---

14. Crucifixion Evidence

In 1968, the bones of a young man who had been crucified during New Testament times were found in the Jerusalem area. The bones were found in a stone box bearing the name "Yehohanan."

Zev Radovan

A 7-inch-long nail was still embedded in the heel bone.

This find shows gruesome evidence of how the Romans crucified persons such as Jesus. Luke 23:33 says, "When they came to the place called the Skull, there they crucified him [Jesus], along with the criminals—one on his right, the other on his left."

Matt Mark Luke

15. Rolling Stone Tombs

At several places in modern Israel there are examples of the type of tomb in which Jesus' body was placed after the Crucifixion. Mostly cut into the sides of hills, each used a large circular stone to cover the entrance.

Inside the tomb is a central room, called an antechamber, and as many as six to eight burial shafts. After the bodies decayed, the bones would be removed from each shaft and placed in a covered stone box (called an ossuary) in the central room. The photograph at right was taken from inside the tomb, looking out past the rolling stone and up the steps.

Below is a tomb with a rolling stone entrance. The curved edge of the stone is on the right. Tombs were mostly cut into the sides of hills and used a large circular stone to roll in front of the entrance. Matthew 27:60; 28:2; Mark 15:46; 16:3, 4; Luke 24:2.

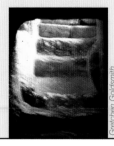

Gretchen Goldsmith

Archaeological Find	Description of the Find	Importance of the Find
The Life and Ministry of Jesus		

The Life and Ministry of Jesus

Matt
Mark
Luke
John

16. Jesus' Burial Place, the Tomb of Joseph of Arimathea

Two different places in Jerusalem have been suggested as the site of the tomb from which Jesus arose. Most archaeologists believe that the Church of the Holy Sepulchre, built around ad 340, stands over the site of the tomb.

Archaeology in and around the Church of the Holy Sepulchre has revealed a rock quarry from the end of the Old Testament era. Tombs had been cut into the quarry wall during the first century ad. The other proposed site for the tomb is the Garden Tomb, or "Gordon's Calvary."

Gretchen Goldsmith

Archaeology in the Garden Tomb area has turned up tombs of the type used during Old Testament times, with some having been reused between ad 400-600. Evidence from both locations may shed new light on the search for this all-important Christian site. Matthew 27:57-60, Mark 15:45-46, Luke 23:50-53, and John 19:38-42 refer to the tomb of Joseph of Arimathea.

Palestine and Trans-Jordan

Matt.
Mark

17. Limestone Ossuary of James

In 2002 a limestone box from the first century ad with the words "James, son of Joseph, brother of Jesus" inscribed on it in Aramaic was found in a private collection in Israel. Matthew 13:55 and Mark 6:3 refer to James, brother of Jesus.

Paul Fisher
The James ossuary was on display at the Royal Ontario Museum from November 15, 2002 to January 5, 2003. Scholars disagree about whether the patina (a film that develops over centuries on stone) in the incisions of the inscriptions chemically matches the patina elsewhere on the ossuary. The history of this ossuary is in debate, as is its authenticity.

The inscription on the box may be the oldest tangible link to Jesus. Of hundreds of these ossuaries, only one other mentions a brother. Scholars suggest that either the brother was responsible for the burial or was prominent. By the ad 60s when James was stoned for his devotion to Jesus as the Messiah, Jesus was prominent, and James was head of the church at Jerusalem.

Matt.
Luke

18. Herodium, King Herod's Palace

Josephus wrote that Herod was buried at his 45-acre palace, called Herodium, about two miles southeast of Bethlehem.

Zev Radovan

In 2007, archaeologists unearthed several fragments of an ornately carved sarcophagus. The sarcophagus is likely the tomb of King Herod.

Matthew 2:19-20 tells of the death of King Herod while the young child Jesus was in Egypt. Matthew 2:1-16 and Luke 1:5 also refer to Herod.

Archaeological Find	Description of the Find	Importance of the Find
Palestine and Trans-Jordan		

19. The Madaba Mosaic Map

This mosaic map of the Holy Land was made about ad 560 to serve as the decorative floor of an early church located near the Dead Sea in modern Jordan.

Gretchen Goldsmith

Portion of Madaba mosaic map

This oldest map of the Holy Land yet found shows the locations of dozens of places where important Biblical events occurred.

20. The Galilee Boat

Matt Mark Luke John

When drought caused the waters of the Sea of Galilee to recede in 1986, residents of a village on the northwest shore found a boat buried in the mud. Later it was removed and restored.

Coins and pottery found with the boat date to New Testament times. The only such boat ever found, it shows what the boats used by Jesus and the disciples were like.

Zev Radovan

The prow of a boat similar to those used by Jesus and his disciples. (Matthew 8:23; Mark 1, 3, 4, 5, 6, 8; Luke 5, 8; John 6:22)

21. Tiberias, Capital City on the Sea of Galilee

John

The modern city of Tiberias stands today over much of the ancient one. However, excavations in 1973-74 revealed two large round stone towers on either side of the main gate dating to the city of Jesus' time.

John McRay

Synagogue floor preserved in Tiberias.

Herod Antipas (one of Herod the Great's sons) founded Tiberias in ad 18 as the capital of Galilee. He was involved in Jesus' trial.

Although Tiberias is mentioned only once in Scripture (John 6:23), it was an important city of the area where Jesus probably carried out much of his ministry.

Archaeological Find	Description of the Find	Importance of the Find
Palestine and Trans-Jordan		
22. Caesarea Philippi Excavations since 1990 have recovered much of the city of Caesarea Philippi from Jesus' day.	A large palace was found which matches Josephus's descriptions of that of Herod Agrippa II, a descendant of Herod the Great. Herod Agrippa II was the governor of Galilee before whom Paul gave a defense of his faith (see Acts 26: 2-29).	According to Matthew 16:13-20 and Mark 8:27-30 Jesus and the disciples were near this city when Jesus asked them who people were saying he was. Peter said, "You are the Christ."
23. Caesarea on the Sea Since the 1950s excavations have turned up most of Herod's harbor, as well as city streets, a theater, the marketplace, shops, aqueducts, temples, and private dwellings.	 *Gretchen Goldsmith* *Caesarea Maritima* Excavations of Caesarea illustrate how important this city was in Jesus' and Paul's day.	Caesarea is where the Apostle Paul first won Gentile converts (Acts 10), and was the site of his imprisonment (Acts 23-26). It was also the home of the Roman governors, such as Pontius Pilate. The city began as Herod's dream and grew into Roman Palestine's major port and governmental center. King Herod Agrippa I was smitten of God in this theater (Acts 12:23).
24. Megiddo (Church Inscription) In 2005, a prayer hall was discovered outside of the Megiddo Prison. The floor of the prayer hall features a detailed mosaic floor with inscriptions that consecrate the church to "God Jesus Christ."	 *Zev Radovan* *This inscription on the mosaic floors consecrates the church to God Jesus Christ. The name of Jesus is identified as being sacred by a line place above it.*	The Bible teaches and the Christian Church has always upheld that Jesus is God (John 1:1-5, 20:28; Hebrews 1:6-8). This find verifies that the Christian Church recognized the divinity of Jesus as early as the third century.

Matt.
Mark
Acts

Acts

Rev.

Archaeological Find	Description of the Find	Importance of the Find
Palestine and Trans-Jordan		

Archaeological Find	Description of the Find	Importance of the Find
25. Sepphoris, Metropolis of Galilee Extensive excavations at Sepphoris have revealed that it was a sizable city built on a Roman plan.	Among the excavated ruins are a large theater, temples, public buildings, and a lavish palace with beautiful mosaics. Although Sepphoris was located only about three miles from Nazareth, it is mentioned nowhere in the New Testament.	Because Sepphoris was very near Nazareth, it is possible that Joseph and the young Jesus could have worked on building projects there. It was also the chief residence of Herod Antipas, who played a role in Jesus' trial in Jerusalem.
Matt. Mark **26. The Ten Cities of the Decapolis** Archaeologists have located almost all ten cities (only the identification of Tell el-Ashari, in Jordan, with Dion remains indefinite). Enough archaeological work has been done to confirm that these were important and wealthy cities in Jesus' day.	 Gretchen Goldsmith *Beth Shean, also known as Sythopolis, one of the Decapolis. (Deca = 10; polis = city)*	Two of the Gospels (Matthew 4:25, Mark 5:20, and 7:31) speak of the spread of Jesus' message among the people of the Decapolis, a league of ten cities where Greek language and culture flourished. One ancient writer lists them as Damascus, Abila, Scythopolis, Hippos, Raphana, Gadara, Pella, Dion, Philadelphia, and Gerasa. For many years the locations of only about half of the cities were known.

Jerusalem and the Temple of Jesus' Day

Archaeological Find	Description of the Find	Importance of the Find
Matt. Mark John **27. Herod's Palace and Pilate's Praetorium in Jerusalem** Since about ad 1100, some pavement north of the Temple Mount has been pointed out as the Praetorium, but archaeologists have found that it dates to about a century after Jesus' and Paul's time.	More recently, archaeologists have identified some Herodian walls, foundations and pavement near the present Jaffa Gate that conform to ancient descriptions of the Praetorium. These remnants can be found today in the vicinity of the Armenian Orthodox Seminary and what is called "the Citadel," or "David's Tower."	Eight passages in the New Testament refer to a place in Jerusalem called in Greek "the Praetorium." In those passages "Praetorium" has been translated as, "the palace courtyard," "the headquarters," "the governor's headquarters," "Pilate's headquarters," "Herod's headquarters," and "the place of the imperial guard." It is where Jesus was brought before Pontius Pilate (Matthew 27:27; Mark 15:16; John 18:28-33).

Archaeological Find	Description of the Find	Importance of the Find
Jerusalem and the Temple of Jesus' Day		

Matt.
Mark
Luke

Archaeological Find	Description of the Find	Importance of the Find
28. The Jerusalem Temple of Jesus' Day (Herod's Temple) Beginning in 1968 excavations commenced in the area of the south retaining wall of the Temple Mount in Jerusalem.	The work has uncovered much of this part of the Temple as it was in Jesus' day, including the southern gates and steps leading up to them.  *Gretchen Goldsmith* At right is the only step on the Temple Mount believed to be from Jesus' day.	It is unknown which entrance to the Temple Mount Jesus and the disciples used in Matthew 21, Mark 11, Luke 19-21, and John 2,5, and 7. Luke 1:9 mentions the priest's custom of burning incense when he went into the Temple of the Lord.
29. "Place of Trumpeting," Temple Inscription from Jesus' Day In 1969 excavators removing debris from the southwest corner of the retaining wall of the ancient Temple in Jerusalem found a rectangular capstone from one of the Temple towers.	*Zev Radovan* *The Hebrew words carved into this Temple tower capstone say, "…to the place of the trumpeting."*	The "place of trumpeting" on the stone refers to the place where the priests blew trumpets announcing the beginnings of holy festivals (See Psalm 81:3 and Joel 2:15). This rare find brings to life the Temple rituals of Jesus' day.
30. A Temple Sundial Relic from Jesus' Day During excavations around Jerusalem's Temple Mount in 1972, excavators found a limestone sundial in a pile of debris left by the Roman army when they destroyed the Temple in AD 70.	Archaeologists discovered that the notches cut into the face of the sundial were carefully calibrated to tell the time and seasons based on the sun's movement in Jerusalem. Carved on its back is a seven-branched menorah (candelabra), like the large one in the Temple. The pile of debris bears testimony to the Roman destruction of the Temple.	Jesus said in Mark 13:2, regarding the Temple, "Not one stone will be left upon another that will not be thrown down" (Matthew 24:2; Luke 21:6). The calibrations on the sundial speak to the importance of correctly measuring both time and the seasons in the priests' performance of the Temple rituals.

Archaeological Find	Description of the Find	Importance of the Find
Jerusalem and the Temple of Jesus' Day		

Acts Eph.

31. Fragments of a Warning to Gentiles from the Temple of Jesus' Day

In 1871 a stone slab containing Greek writing surfaced in Jerusalem. In 1938 another slab similar to it was found just north of the Temple Mount. Both translate, "No gentile may enter within this Temple barrier! Anyone caught will be responsible for his own death."

Zev Radovan

Stone slab with Greek writing gives warning that Gentiles should not enter the Temple. (In Acts 21:27-29 the Jews accused Paul of bringing Greeks into the Temple.)

According to Josephus, a Jewish writer of the first century, these warnings were hung on a low wall that divided the public square of the Temple from the sacred inner courtyard that was accessible only to Jews. These rare finds from the Temple of Jesus' day shed light on the Temple regulations, and enrich our understanding of the importance of Ephesians 2:14, "For he [Jesus] is our peace, who has made us both one, and has broken down the dividing wall of hostility."

Mark Luke Hebrews

32. The Holy of Holies in the Temple of Jesus' Day

Archaeologist and leading authority on the Temple, Leen Ritmeyer, has now found what appear to be the foundations of the walls of the Holy of Holies (the most sacred portion) of the ancient Temple.

The Temple was completely destroyed by the Romans in AD 70. Six centuries later the Muslims built a shrine called the Dome of the Rock on the vacant Temple Mount (right). Many scholars conclude that the exact location of the Temple can no longer be found. However, in the bedrock beneath the Dome of the Rock, trenches were discovered, cut into the rock. Photo shot from above.

The trenches conform precisely to the dimensions of the walls of the Holy of Holies, as described in ancient Jewish writings. Finding the trenches that match the dimensions of the walls of the Holy of Holies could well provide the location of the events recorded in Mark 15:38 and Luke 23:45 (the veil of the Temple was torn in two from top to bottom when Jesus died). The Holy of Holies is mentioned in Hebrews 6:19, 9:3-11, 10:20.

Mark Luke

33. The Arch of Titus

Carved in relief on the triumphal Arch of Titus, in the ancient Forum (public square) of Rome, is a scene of Roman soldiers on parade carrying the sacred items looted from the Temple in Jerusalem in ad 70. These items included the Table of the Showbread, the Menorah (Golden Lampstand), and a scroll of God's Law.

John McRay

Between Christ's resurrection and the time when Christianity was spreading throughout the Mediterranean world, a cataclysmic event occurred—the Roman army, under General Titus, invaded Jerusalem. On the ninth of Av (a Jewish calendar month corresponding to June) in ad 70, the army destroyed both the city and the Temple, carrying away the sacred Temple items. In the ancient Forum in the city of Rome there still stands a triumphal archway commemorating the victory of Titus and his army. See Mark 13:2; Luke 2:16.

Archaeological Find	Description of the Find	Importance of the Find
	The Ministry of Paul	

The Ministry of Paul

34. Damascus, City of Saul's Conversion

Located in Syria, modern Damascus covers most of the ancient city today. Limited excavations have revealed some of the city's Roman gates, arches, and even the remains of "the street called Straight," where Saul stayed during his sojourn in the city (Acts 9:11).

John McRay
Straight Street in modern Damascus.

Though first mentioned in the Bible in Genesis 14:15, Damascus is important also in the New Testament as the site of the conversion and early witness of Saul (Paul), as recorded in Acts 9:1-25. This reference reveals that Saul stayed at a home located on the main east-west road, near the heart of the city.

35. The Politarch Inscriptions

Thirty-two inscriptions have been found that have the term "politarchs" ("city authorities"), and 19 of them come from Thessalonica. At least three inscriptions date from Paul's time.

Because the Greek term "politarchs" could not be found in existing ancient literature outside of the New Testament, some critics argued that Luke must have been mistaken in his use of the term in Acts 17:6. That passage speaks of some believers at Thessalonica being dragged by a mob before the "politarchs." At least three inscriptions date from Paul's time, showing that Luke was quite correct in this detail.

36. The Areopagus at Athens

Gretchen Goldsmith

Areopagus (Mars Hill) in Athens, Greece

Archaeological investigations have located two terraces linked by steps on the hill. The upper terrace has a long rock-cut bench designed for seating many people. Since early Christian times, a hill in the heart of Athens, immediately west of the Acropolis, has been referred to as the Areopagus.

Acts 17:19-34 gives the account of Paul's presentation of the Gospel before the Athenian administrative council, known as the Areopagus. The term "Areopagus" is Greek for "Hill of Ares (or Mars)." The council seems to have taken its name from the place where they met.

Acts

Archaeological Find	Description of the Find	Importance of the Find
The Ministry of Paul		

37. The Gallio Inscription

Archaeologists found a stone inscription at Delphi, in Greece, that mentions a Roman governor (proconsul) named Gallio of the province of Achaia.

Gretchen Goldsmith

This inscription contains a Roman date, corresponding to 52 AD. The name "Gallio" is highlighted.

Gallio is the same governor referred to in Acts 18:12. The date on this inscription allows Bible scholars to know almost exactly when the Apostle Paul was ministering to early Christians in Corinth.

38. The Bema at Corinth

One of the most important New Testament archaeological finds from Corinth is the city's "Bema," a platform where officials addressed the public.

Gretchen Goldsmith

Wall at right is the platform on which the Bema was built. Spectators stood about 7.5 feet below on stone pavement.

In AD 51 the Apostle Paul was brought before the Roman governor Gallio at this platform in Corinth (Acts 18:12-17). The Bema was discovered in 1935. The identity of the Bema is certain because of seven pieces of an inscription found nearby.

39. Ephesus, Jewel of Asia Minor

Arvel Witte

Archaeology has recovered much of the city of Ephesus from Paul's day. The temple of Artemis, one of the seven wonders of the ancient world, has been located. Also found was the theater where Paul's companions were dragged during a riot of silversmiths resulting from Paul's preaching (Acts 19:23-41).

This large city was the place the Apostle Paul stayed the longest during his missionary journeys (Acts 18:19-21 and 19:1-41). The letter to the Ephesians was written to the believers at Ephesus by Paul.

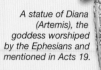

A statue of Diana (Artemis), the goddess worshiped by the Ephesians and mentioned in Acts 19.

Gretchen Goldsmith

Archaeological Find	Description of the Find	Importance of the Find
The Ministry of Paul		

The Ministry of Paul

Romans **40. The Erastus Inscription** In 1929 archaeologists found a paving stone near the theater of Corinth in Greece that contains Erastus's name, and notes that he was indeed a Roman public official there.	Writing from Corinth, the Apostle Paul passed along greetings from several Corinthian believers, including Erastus, the city treasurer or chamberlain (Romans 16:23). This find, with seven inch high letters, verifies Erastus's existence as a public official in Corinth just as the Bible says.	 *Erastus's name on paving stone. Foot at top shows size.*

Early Christianity in the Mediterranean World

Acts **41. Antioch, Important Center of Early Christianity** Artifacts found in Antioch (in Turkey today) reveal that the city had a population that was diverse racially and ethnically. It was an important crossroad in the immense Roman highway system. In New Testament times Antioch grew to be second only to Jerusalem as a large center of Christianity.	 *Arvel Witte* *Modern Antakya, Turkey* Excavations have shown that Antioch was a large Roman city in Paul's day covered today by the Turkish city of Antakya.	Acts 11 and 14 recount the work of Paul and Barnabas in Antioch helping to build a Christian community made up of people from a wide variety of backgrounds. These finds help to explain why the establishment of the strong body of believers at Antioch played such a vital role in the future spread of Christianity throughout the entire Mediterranean region.
Acts Phil **42. Philippi, Where Paul First Preached in Europe** Among the ruins at Philippi are numerous carved shrines to various Greco-Roman and eastern gods and goddesses. On top of the city's acropolis (highest hill) are the remains of ramparts (defensive walls) and a theater.	 *Gretchen Goldsmith* *Excavated area of the Roman forum in Philippi.*	Located in northeast Greece, Philippi is where Paul preached his first sermon on European soil, and won a convert in Lydia, "a seller of purple" (see Acts 16:12-14). Paul wrote a letter to the Philippians.  *The Via Egnatia, an important east-west Roman highway that passed through this significant early seat of Christianity.*

Archaeological Find	Description of the Find	Importance of the Find
Early Christianity in the Mediterranean World		
43. Thessalonica, Capital of Macedonia Located about 115 miles southwest of Philippi, along the ancient Roman highway known as the Via Egnatia, lies the city of Thessalonica. The Via Egnatia was an important east-west Roman highway that passed through this area.	Archaeological remains include the remnants of several early church buildings, a Roman triumphal arch, and some of the city's ancient walls. Little is seen here from the time of Paul because modern Salonika, the second largest city in Greece, covers the buried remains of Roman Thessalonica.	According to Acts 17:1-10 Paul visited here, preaching three times in the synagogue. He was subsequently expelled from the city. Still, he persisted in planting a church, and eventually wrote two epistles to the Christians there. Thessalonica went on to become an important center of early Christianity, with several churches.
44. "God Fearers" Inscriptions At the ancient sites of Aphrodisias and Miletus in modern Turkey, scholars have discovered two interesting inscriptions carved in marble and placed at ancient public buildings.	Each inscription contains the term "God Fearers" with reference to a group identified by outsiders as being a part of the Jews.	This term is much the same as what is found in Acts 13:16, 26, 43, and Acts 17:4, 17 where the meaning has puzzled scholars for a long time. The inscriptions show that the God Fearers likely were non-Jews who believed in the God of Israel.
45. Seven Churches of Revelation Archaeological excavations have now been carried out at all seven ancient cities, and the work at Ephesus, Smyrna, Pergamum, and Sardis in particular has been very extensive.	 *photo credit: Arvel Witte* Little remains of Smyrna from the New Testament period. Today the city of Izmir in Turkey covers Smyrna's remains.	In Revelation 1:11 John is instructed by the Lord to send messages to seven churches in the Roman province of Asia, located in western Turkey today. Revelation 2 and 3 contain the messages addressed to the churches at Ephesus, Smyrna, Pergamum, Thyatira, Sardis, Philadelphia, and Laodicea.

Acts
1 Thes.
2 Thes.

Acts

Rev.

Archaeological Find	Description of the Find	Importance of the Find
Ancient Manuscripts		
46. The Dead Sea Scrolls These finds, including both entire ancient scrolls and scraps of them, were found mostly in caves along the northwest shore of the Dead Sea. In 1947 shepherds found the first seven scrolls stuffed in ancient pottery jars in a cave.	Practically all of the Dead Sea scrolls are written in Hebrew and Aramaic. Among them are the oldest copies yet found of almost all of the books of the Old Testament. They date from between about 300 BC to AD 70. Also of special significance are the non-biblical documents, which reveal much about the varied nature of Judaism during the time between the Old and New Testament periods.	 Gretchen Goldsmith *One of the eleven caves in the Qumran area, about seven miles south of Jericho, where the scrolls were found. These scrolls were important for shedding light on the Bible.*
47. Earliest New Testament Copy In 1920 a British traveler in Egypt acquired a small fragment of papyrus (a paperlike substance made from woven reed stalks). Later, scholars discovered that the writing on it was from the Gospel of John.	 Rick Humphrey *An illustration of the oldest New Testament fragment yet found. The words on it are from John 18:31-33, 37-38. It was part of a codex dated AD 125. It is known as the John Rylands Papyrus and is in the John Rylands Library in Manchester, England.*	Because no originals of the biblical books have survived, scholars have relied on the finds of ancient copies to piece together the text of the Bible. The papyrus codex was likely copied within a generation of the original book of John itself.
48. Oldest Copy of John's Gospel In 1956 the world learned of the existence of a copy of the Gospel of John that had been penned in Greek on papyrus sometime between AD 150-200.	Hailed as the oldest remaining copy of the majority of John's Gospel, about two-thirds of the text has survived the ravages of time. Swiss industrialist M. Martin Bodmer purchased it in Egypt, and later gave it to a museum.	This early copy has proved invaluable to Bible scholars and translators for helping to reconstruct the most accurate Greek text possible of the Gospel of John.

Archaeological Find	Description of the Find	Importance of the Find
Ancient Manuscripts		
49. The Oldest Complete Copy of the New Testament In 1844 New Testament scholar Konstantin von Tischendorf discovered the oldest surviving copy of the New Testament. He found it among the books belonging to a monastery that has stood at the foot of Mount Sinai since ancient times.	Known today as Codex Sinaiticus, this Bible was written on parchment around AD 350. This text is also known by the name "'Aleph," the Hebrew letter "A." The other early key Greek text is Codex Vaticanus, also known as "B." *Drawing of parchment codex made from fine quality skins of sheep or goats.* 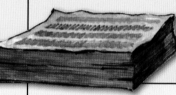	Codex Sinaiticus has proved vital to scholars and translators in verifying the accuracy with which the New Testament has been reproduced across the ages. When new Bible versions refer to "most reliable texts," they are referring to "A" and "B."
50. Greco-Roman References to Jesus Flavius Josephus, Jewish historian, wrote *Antiquities* (AD 93), which mentions both Jesus and his brothers. Tacitus wrote *Annals* between ad 115-117, which mentions Jesus' execution by Pilate.	*Antiquities* states "About this time arose Jesus, a wise man. For he was a doer of marvelous deeds, and a teacher of men who gladly receive the truth. He drew to himself many persons, both of the Jews and also of the Gentiles. And when Pilate, upon the indictment of the leading men among us, had condemned him to the cross, those who had loved him at first did not cease to do so. And even to this day the race of Christians, who are named from him, has not died out."	Tacitus's *Annals* state "Christus, from whom the name [Christians] had its origin, suffered the extreme penalty during the reign of Tiberias at the hand of one of our procurators, Pontius Pilate, and a deadly superstition, thus checked for the moment, again broke out not only in Judaea, the first source of the evil, but also in the City..."

Contributor: Professor Larry McKinney, Central Baptist Theological Seminary, Kansas.

Special thanks to Dr. John McRay, Wheaton College, and Michael Cochrane.

Arrangement of Events
The contents of this chart are generally arranged from the earliest events mentioned in the Bible to the most recent events.

Dates of Events (examples)
1st century AD = AD 1-100
2nd century AD = AD 101-200
10th century AD = AD 901-1000
13th century AD = AD 1201-1300
1st millennium AD = AD 1-1000
2nd millennium AD = AD 1001-2000

Why Trust the Bible?

Was the Bible Tampered With?

How Do We Know the Bible was Copied Accurately?

Answers to the New Critics

Can the Bible Be Trusted?

Before the invention of the printing press, scribes copied the Scriptures by hand for more than one thousand years —

♦ without eyeglasses

♦ by the light of candles

♦ using quill pens and ground charcoal mixed with gum and water to scratch the sacred words of Scripture on rough papyrus and vellum

What if these scribes got it wrong?

Some recent bestselling books — such as Bart Ehrman's *Misquoting Jesus* — argue that the scribes *did* get it wrong. Here's a summary of recent claims about the surviving manuscripts of the Bible: "Not only do we not have the originals [of the biblical manuscripts], we don't have the first copies of the originals. We have only error-ridden copies, and the vast majority of these are centuries removed from the originals and different from them in thousands of ways. Mistakes multiply and get repeated; sometimes they get corrected and sometimes they get compounded. And so it goes. For centuries. In some places, we simply cannot be sure that we have reconstructed the text accurately. It's a bit hard to know what the words of the Bible mean if we don't even know what the words are."[1]

Thousands of people read and believe these attacks on the Bible. Still, millions of people continue to trust the Bible as an authoritative, written record that conveys consistent and reliable truth about God. So which is it?

Does the Bible still convey the truths that the original authors intended? Or were the ancient texts changed with such reckless abandon that contemporary biblical scholars are left with manuscripts so "error-ridden" they can't even be certain what the texts originally meant?

With these questions in mind, let's look at the history of the biblical texts to see what the historical record actually tells us!

Here's what we'll find:

♦ The Bible can be trusted.

♦ We can know what the Bible says.

♦ We can be confident that our Bible today is faithful to the original manuscripts, despite differences that exist in ancient copies.

GOSPEL	DATE (APPROXIMATE)	SOURCE
MARK	AD 65	Peter, written by Mark
MATTHEW	AD 75	Matthew
LUKE	AD 75	Luke, a companion of Paul
JOHN	AD 90	John

How Were the Stories Passed Down?

■ What the skeptics claim:

"[The Gospels] were written thirty-five to sixty-five years after Jesus' death, . . . not by people who were eyewitnesses, but by people living later."[2]

■ What history actually tells us:

Yes and no. While it's true that the Gospels were probably written between thirty-five and sixty-five years after the death of Jesus, historical evidence strongly suggests that the sources of the New Testament Gospels were eyewitnesses of the events of Jesus' life. Mark's Gospel emerged around AD 65; the Gospels According to Matthew and Luke began to circulate a decade or so later. John's Gospel seems to have been penned around AD 90. Even with these dates, it is at least *possible* that the sources of these books were eyewitnesses of Jesus. The emergence of Mark's Gospel only thirty years or so after Jesus' death makes it unreasonable to deny that the Gospels, at the very least, *could* have been written by eyewitnesses.[3]

(Courtesy of CSNTM.org)

In ancient epistles, the author's name appeared at the beginning of the letter, as in this copy of Paul's letter to the Romans. In ancient historical writings—such as the Gospels—the author's name was sometimes omitted.

What matters most, though, isn't *when* the Gospels were written. *What matters most is whether the Gospels accurately represent eyewitness accounts of the life and ministry of Jesus.* According to ancient recollections from such early Christian leaders as Papias of Hierapolis, Polycarp of Smyrna, and Irenaeus of Lyons, each of the four New Testament Gospels represents eyewitness testimony about Jesus Christ. According to these recollections—recollections that bear every mark of originating in the first century AD—

- The anecdotes recorded in the Gospel According to Mark are the testimony of Peter, preserved in written form by his translator Mark.

- Luke's Gospel integrates written and oral sources gathered from eyewitnesses by Paul's personal physician, Luke.

- The materials that are unique to the Gospel According to Matthew came from Matthew, a tax collector who deserted a profitable profession to follow Jesus.

- The accounts in the Gospel According to John find their source in the apostle John.[4]

■ What the skeptics claim:

"Stories based on eyewitness accounts are not necessarily reliable, and the same is true a hundredfold for accounts that . . . have been in oral circulation long after the fact."[5]

■ What history actually tells us:

In a culture that passed on information orally—such as the biblical world—it was possible for oral histories to remain reliable for remarkably long periods of time. People in today's world—surrounded by high levels of literacy and easy access to writing materials—are accustomed to recording important information in *written form*. But, especially among the ancient Jews, important teachings were told and retold in rhythmic, repetitive patterns so that students could memorize key truths.[6] These teachings were known as *oral histories*. In these forms, it was possible for teachings and accounts of historical events to remain amazingly consistent from one generation to the next.[7] Much of the Old Testament and some portions of the New Testament—for example, the eyewitness accounts mentioned in Luke 1:2—may have been passed down as reliable oral histories before they were written.

■ What the skeptics claim:

Stories in the New Testament "were changed with what would strike us today as reckless abandon. They were modified, amplified, and embellished. And sometimes they were made up."[8]

■ What history actually tells us:

The New Testament accounts of Jesus were not made up or changed with "reckless abandon." Consistent oral histories about the life of Jesus and the early church emerged among eyewitnesses shortly after the events occurred; these oral histories remained consistent as they spread across the Roman Empire.

As an example, let's take a look at one of these segments of oral history, recorded in written form in 1 Corinthians 15:3-7.[9] How do we know that these words from the apostle Paul represent part of the oral tradition about Jesus? Paul introduced this summation with two Greek words—*paradidomi* ("handed over" or "delivered") and *paralambano* ("received")—that indicated it was oral tradition. Ancient readers understood these two words, when used together, to imply that the writer was citing oral history.[10]

A quick examination of these verses demonstrates how quickly oral histories emerged among the eyewitnesses of Jesus

The word "canon" comes from the Greek word *kanon*, which meant "measuring stick." In the fourth century AD, the writings that Christians accepted as authoritative began to be known as a "canon" because these witnesses measured the church's faithfulness to Jesus Christ. Christians embraced the Jewish canon—the books known to us as "the Old Testament"—because they believed that the God of the Jewish Scriptures was also the Father of Jesus Christ. Each writing in the New Testament was expected to be connected to an eyewitness of the risen Lord, to be recognized in churches throughout the known world, and not to contradict other writings about Jesus.

This painting from the ruins of Pompeii shows how widely wax tablets and styluses were used to record thoughts in written form.

and how consistent these traditions remained. Even though Paul wrote in Greek, he called the apostle Peter by his Aramaic name, "Cephas." Then, there's the repeated phrase "and that." The phrase rendered "and that" is the Greek translation of an Aramaic method for joining clauses.[11] Based on the grammatical patterns in these verses, it's clear that this oral history originally circulated in Aramaic. And where did people speak Aramaic? In Galilee and Judea, the places where Jesus walked and talked, died and rose from the dead! And when could Paul have received an oral history of the death and resurrection of Jesus in Aramaic? The point at which Paul seems to have learned this version of the historical account was around AD 35 when he visited Jerusalem and heard the story of Jesus from an eyewitness (Galatians 1:18). For Paul to have received a consistent oral history in Aramaic at this time, scholars estimate that this account—a tradition that clearly affirms the essential facts of Jesus' resurrection—first surfaced near Jerusalem shortly after Jesus was crucified.[12]

From this bit of oral history, it's clear that the earliest Christians did *not* recklessly alter their traditions. Otherwise, how could Paul—writing three years after he first visited Corinth—have said to the Corinthians immediately before he quoted this oral history, "I am reminding you, brothers, about the good proclamation that I proclaimed to you," suggesting that Paul proclaimed similar words in each place that he visited? (1 Corinthians 15:1). Clearly, this example from the oral accounts of Jesus' life was *not* "made up" long after the events or "changed with . . . reckless abandon," as the skeptics claim. To the contrary, this oral tradition about Jesus emerged soon after his resurrection and remained relatively unchanged as it spread across the Roman Empire.

(Courtesy of the Schøyen Collection, Oslo and London)

This summary from a medical manual, copied shortly before the time of Jesus, demonstrates some level of literacy among first-century physicians such as Luke.

■ What the skeptics claim:

"There is not a sentence concerning Jesus in the entire New Testament composed by anyone who had ever met the unwilling King of the Jews."[13] "Jesus' own followers . . . were mainly lower-class peasants—fishermen and artisans, for example—and . . . they spoke Aramaic rather than Greek. . . . In the end, it seems unlikely that the uneducated, lower-class, illiterate disciples of Jesus played the decisive role in the literary compositions that have come down through history under their names."[14]

■ What history actually tells us:

Not all of Jesus' first followers were illiterate; even if some followers *were* illiterate, professional scribes—people who were capable of turning oral histories into polished Greek—were readily available even to working-class persons.

In the book that bears the name "Matthew," the apostle Matthew is presented as a tax collector (Matthew 10:3). It's unlikely that any early Christian would have fabricated this bit of vocational trivia. Since Roman governors expected tax collectors to stockpile personal wealth by cheating people, tax collectors rarely made it to the top of anyone's list of most-loved citizens. But there was one skill that tax collectors *did* possess. *They could read and write.* Tax collectors carried *pinakes*, hinged wooden tablets with beeswax coating on each panel.[15] Tax collectors etched notes in the wax using styluses; these notes could be translated later and rewritten on papyrus.[16] Papyri from Egypt prove that tax collectors also wrote receipts for citizens in their villages.[17] So, a tax collector such as Matthew could *not* have been illiterate. The daily tasks of a Galilean tax collector required him to copy and record information in multiple languages.

What about another character whose name is ascribed to a Gospel, the companion of Paul named "Luke"? Compared to other people in the New Testament, Luke is a quite obscure character. He's mentioned only three times in letters attributed to Paul (Colossians 4:14; Philemon 1:24; 2 Timothy 4:11). Considering how many of Paul's partners enjoy far greater prominence in the New Testament—Timothy, for example, or Barnabas or Silas—it's difficult to explain why anyone would ascribe the third Gospel to Luke…unless, of course, Luke actually *was* responsible for the book that bears his name.

(Courtesy of CSNTM.org)

According to Colossians 4:14, Luke was Paul's "beloved physician." Ancient physicians seem to have possessed, at least, the capacity to read the summaries of medical knowledge that flourished in the first century. Papyri from Egypt prove that many physicians also wrote reports for law-enforcement officials regarding suspicious injuries, as well as statements for slave-masters certifying the health of slaves.[18] So, it's unlikely that Luke was completely "illiterate." What's more, many physicians could pull together various eyewitness accounts into coherent reports, just as the preface of Luke's Gospel suggests that the author has done (Luke 1:1-4).

John Rylands Papyrus 52 records portions of John 18. The writing style and material suggest that this fragment was copied around AD 110.

That leaves Mark and John. Though it is by no means certain, these men *may* have been illiterate. Still, in the first century AD, professional scribes were readily available to render messages from other languages, including Aramaic, into polished Greek. Complex legal titles, epistles to family members, and simple commercial receipts all required secretarial skills—and provided livelihoods for a multitude of scribes.[19] Even though Paul was completely capable of writing in Greek (Galatians 6:11; Philemon 1:19-21), scribes penned Paul's letters for him (Romans 16:22; see also 1 Peter 5:12).[20] It's entirely possible that Mark and John employed professional scribes to render their oral accounts of Jesus' life into Greek documents. If so, they would still have been the *sources* of these Gospels.[21]

How Can We Know that the Bible was Copied Accurately?

■ What the skeptics claim:

"The [Old Testament] is filled with lots of textual problems—as we have come to realize, for example, with the discovery of the Dead Sea Scrolls."[22]

■ What history actually tells us:

In truth, the Dead Sea Scrolls proved the precise opposite. The Dead Sea Scrolls demonstrated how carefully the Old Testament had been copied through the centuries. Around AD 900—nearly a millennium after the time of Jesus—groups of Jewish scribes known as Masoretes began to copy the Old Testament texts according to strict guidelines. The Masoretes maintained nearly perfect accuracy in their copies. Until the discovery of the Dead Sea Scrolls, these Masoretic texts were the oldest available manuscripts of the Old Testament. When the Dead Sea Scrolls were unearthed in the mid-twentieth century, scholars compared the text of Isaiah from the Dead Sea Scrolls with the text of Isaiah preserved by the Masoretes. What these scholars discovered was that—even though more than 1,000 years separated the Dead Sea Scrolls from the Masoretic texts—the Dead Sea Scrolls and the Masoretic texts agreed word-for-word more than 95% of the time![23] The remaining differences stemmed primarily from minor spelling variations. Even the scrolls that differ a bit more than the Isaiah scrolls—for example, the copies of 1 and 2 Samuel and Deuteronomy—do not differ in any way that affects any crucial Jewish or Christian belief.

> *Sir Frederic Kenyon,* former director of the British Museum, commented concerning the Gospels, "The interval between the dates of the original composition and the earliest extant evidence [is] so small as to be negligible, and the last foundation for any doubt that the Scriptures have come down to us substantially as they were written has now been removed."[37]

■ What the skeptics claim:

"There are more differences among our manuscripts than there are words in the New Testament.... We have only error-ridden copies, and the vast majority of these are centuries removed from the originals and different from them…in thousands of ways."[24]

■ What history actually tells us:

More than ninety-nine percent of the variants in the New Testament are not even noticeable when the text is translated; of the remaining differences, *none* affects any vital aspect of Christian faith.[25]

Scholars have 5,700 or so ancient biblical manuscripts available to them. Although many of these manuscripts include the entire New Testament, most are partial copies, found in fragmented form in the sands of Egypt or in the monasteries of Europe and western Asia. All totaled, these manuscripts include more than two million pages of text. In these two-million-plus pages of biblical text, there are between 200,000 and 400,000 variations in wording or spelling. In a complete Greek New Testament, there are approximately 138,000 words. So, yes, there *are* more differences among the total manuscripts than there are words in one complete Greek New Testament. What the skeptics don't clearly communicate to their readers, though, is *the sheer insignificance of these variants.*

(Courtesy of the Schøyen Collection, Oslo and London)

Most of these 400,000 variations stem from differences in spelling, word order, or the relationships between nouns and definite articles—slight variants that are easily recognizable. After minor spelling errors and slight variations in word order are factored out, there is more than 99% agreement between all of the known manuscripts of the Bible! Of the remaining variants, none affects any crucial element of the Christian faith.

■ What the skeptics claim:

"Scribes who were not altogether satisfied with what the New Testament books said modified their words to make them … more vigorously oppose heretics, women, Jews, and pagans."[26]

■ What history actually tells us:

With more than 5,700 manuscripts and fragments of the New Testament available to us, it would be impossible for anyone to have modified major portions the New Testament without their changes being quite easily noticed. In the few cases when changes *were* attempted, the original text can—in all but the tiniest handful of instances—be easily restored by examining the most ancient New Testament manuscripts.[27]

Some scribes after the New Testament era may have altered texts that placed women in prominent positions. For example, in Romans 16:7, someone named Junia—a name that appears to be feminine—is said to be "significant among the apostles," but a later scribe seems to have turned "Junia" into "Junias," a man's name.[28] In the most ancient manuscripts of Acts 18:26, a woman named Priscilla

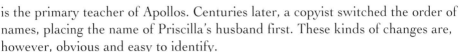

is the primary teacher of Apollos. Centuries later, a copyist switched the order of names, placing the name of Priscilla's husband first. These kinds of changes are, however, obvious and easy to identify.

WORKS OF PLATO	NEW TESTAMENT
• Written around 400 BC • Only seven copies have survived • The earliest surviving manuscript was copied between AD 800 and 900 — more than 1,200 years after the original documents were written	• Written between AD 60 and 100 • More than 5,700 portions have survived • Complete manuscripts of the New Testament have survived from the late third or early fourth centuries — less than three centuries after the original documents were written • Hundreds of fragments and manuscripts have survived from the second, third, and fourth centuries

Even in the very few cases that remain uncertain, the problem is not with the texts themselves. The difficulty is with the choices of individuals to twist biblical texts to sanction negative attitudes toward women, Jews, or non-believers. In any case, the claim that the Bible as we have it today has been modified for the purpose of opposing women, Jews, and pagans has no substantive foundation in the actual texts.

■ What the skeptics claim:

"Many of our cherished biblical stories and widely held beliefs concerning the divinity of Jesus, the Trinity, and the divine origins of the Bible itself stem from both intentional and accidental alterations by scribes."[29]

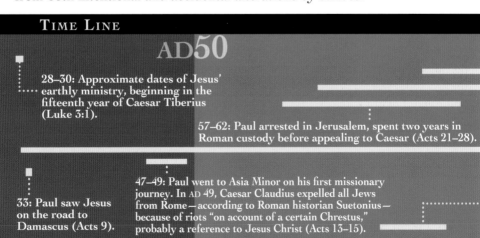

TIME LINE

AD50

28–30: Approximate dates of Jesus' earthly ministry, beginning in the fifteenth year of Caesar Tiberius (Luke 3:1).

57–62: Paul arrested in Jerusalem, spent two years in Roman custody before appealing to Caesar (Acts 21–28).

33: Paul saw Jesus on the road to Damascus (Acts 9).

47–49: Paul went to Asia Minor on his first missionary journey. In AD 49, Caesar Claudius expelled all Jews from Rome — according to Roman historian Suetonius — because of riots "on account of a certain Chrestus," probably a reference to Jesus Christ (Acts 13–15).

■ **What history actually tells us:**

This claim is simply not true. Firm belief in the divinity of the Jesus, the threefold nature of God, and the divine origins of the Bible emerged among Christians before the New Testament was even completed. None of these beliefs depends on disputed or altered passages in the Bible. It is true that one verse that mentions the Trinity was not originally present in the biblical text: The last half of 1 John 5:7—a text that, in some later manuscripts, reads, "There are three that testify in heaven, the Father, the Word, and the Spirit, and these three are one"—doesn't appear in the most ancient New Testament manuscripts. But the doctrine of the Trinity does not depend on this verse. God's nature as three-yet-one is affirmed just as clearly in Matthew 28:19, where Jesus commanded his followers to baptize in the *name* (singular) of the Father, Son, and Spirit. Similarly, the most ancient copies of 1 Timothy 3:16 declare, "Great is the mystery of godliness; he was manifested in the flesh," while a few later texts read, "*God* was manifested in the flesh." But, again, the doctrine of the deity of Jesus does *not* depend on this text; the deity of Jesus is clearly affirmed in several undisputed texts, including John 20:28, where Thomas recognized Jesus as Lord and God. No essential Christian belief is affected by any variant in the biblical manuscripts.

Who Chose the Books in My Bible?

■ **What the skeptics claim:**

"Many Christians today may think that the canon of the New Testament simply appeared on the scene one day, soon after the death of Jesus, but nothing could be farther from the truth. As it turns out, we are able to pinpoint the first time that any Christian of record listed the twenty-seven books of our New Testament as *the* books of the New Testament—neither more nor fewer. ... In the year 367, Athanasius wrote his annual pastoral letter to the Egyptian churches under his jurisdiction, and in it he ... lists our twenty-seven books, excluding all others."[30]

TIME LINE

AD100

c. 35–c. 117: Ignatius of Antioch was a disciple of John, the author of the Gospel; he wrote seven letters to churches as he traveled to Rome to suffer martyrdom during the reign of Emperor Trajan. In these letters, he quoted sayings that are found in Gospels of Matthew and Luke as well as Acts, Romans, 1 Corinthians, Ephesians, Colossians, and 1 Thessalonians.[36] These quotations demonstrate that early Christians treated these texts as authoritative. ·········•

66–70: After years of enduring oppression from Roman governors, the Jews revolted. Their rebellion resulted in the destruction of the Jewish temple in AD 70.

■ What history actually tells us:

This statement leaves out several key facts about the selection of the New Testament books. It is true that Athanasius was the first author to list the exact same twenty-seven books that we find in the New Testament today. Yet, from the beginning, Christians unanimously accepted the four Gospels, Acts, Paul's letters, and the first epistle of John. Although disputes about a few New Testament books lasted into the fourth century, widespread agreement about which writings were authoritative existed among Christians from the first century onward. The primary standard for deciding which books were authoritative emerged long before the fourth century—and the standard *wasn't* the word of a powerful bishop. Hints of this standard can, in fact, be found in Christian writings of the first century AD. The basic idea was this: *Testimony that could be connected to eyewitnesses of the risen Lord was uniquely authoritative*

among early Christians.[31] From the beginning, authoritative testimony about Jesus Christ had to have its source in eyewitnesses of the risen Lord. Even while the New Testament books were being written, the words of people who saw and followed the risen Lord carried special weight in the churches (see Acts 1:21-26; 15:6—16:5; 1 Corinthians 4—5; 9:1-12; Galatians 1:1-12; 1 Thessalonians 5:26-27). The logic of this standard was simple: The people most likely to know the truth about Jesus were eyewitnesses who had encountered Jesus personally or their close associates.

(Courtesy of the Schøyen Collection, Oslo and London)

The sermons of the third-century theologian Origen of Alexandria clearly recognized the authority of the New Testament writings.

Although debates continued into the fourth century about a few writings—including the letters of Peter, John's second and third letters, and the letters of James and Jude—Christians universally agreed at least as early as the second century on the authority of no fewer than nineteen of the books in the New Testament—and these are the writings that reflect some of the most essential truths about Jesus. Even if this score or so of books had been the only documents that represented eyewitness testimony about Jesus, every vital truth of Christian faith would remain completely intact. What directed this process was the conviction that these writings must be rooted in reliable, eyewitness testimony about Jesus Christ.

TIME LINE

AD150

c. 69–c. 155: Polycarp of Smyrna was a disciple of John, the author of the Gospel. In 155 or 156, Polycarp suffered martyrdom for his faith.

c. 60–c. 135: Papias of Hierapolis was a disciple of John, the author of the Gospel; Papias recorded several ancient traditions about the origins of the Gospels.

When deciding which Old Testament writings to accept, Christians embraced the same listing of books as the Jewish people. When the Septuagint—a popular Greek-language version of the Jewish holy writings—was translated around 200 BC, the translators had included some Jewish writings which never appeared in the Hebrew Scriptures and which Jewish rabbis rejected around AD 90 at the Council of Jamnia (Yavneh). The Roman Catholic and Eastern Orthodox Churches recognize these additional books from the Septuagint as authoritative; these writings appear in the Roman Catholic and Eastern Orthodox Bibles as "deuterocanonical" or "apocryphal" books.

■ What the skeptics claim:

Among the earliest Christians, "there was no agreed-upon canon—and no agreed-upon theology. Instead, there was a wide range of diversity: diverse groups asserting diverse theologies based on diverse written texts, all claiming to be written by apostles of Jesus."[32]

■ What history actually tells us:

Among the people who walked and talked with Jesus, a consensus emerged very early regarding both the identity of Jesus and all but a few biblical books. It's true that there *were* several divergent sets of beliefs that circulated within the earliest churches. It's also true that debates about a few biblical books lasted beyond the first and second centuries. Yet the persons who actually walked and talked with Jesus agreed about the nature of Jesus even before the New Testament was completed. Consensus about all but a few New Testament books was reached by the mid-second century, probably earlier. According to the records found in the New Testament—the only writings about Jesus that were written early enough to be connected to eyewitnesses of Jesus—Jesus was human and yet divine, he was the messianic king predicted in the Hebrew Scriptures, he was physically raised from the dead, and it is only by trusting in him that anyone can enjoy the life that God created humanity to live, both now and in eternity (see Jn. 20:28-31; 1 Cor. 15:1-7; 1 Jn. 2:22; 4:1-3). According to the eyewitnesses of Jesus, to deny such truths as these was to exclude oneself from fellowship with Jesus Christ and with his followers (see 1 Jn. 4:1-6).

TIME LINE

AD200

........130–202: Irenaeus of Lyons repeated the same traditions that Papias reported nearly a century earlier, adding, "The heretics boast that they have many more gospels than there really are. ... But there are only four authentic gospels. These alone were written by Jesus' true followers."

(Courtesy of CSNTM.org)

This painting of the apostle John appears at the beginning of John's Gospel in a thirteenth-century manuscript.

How Reliable is My Bible?

■ What the skeptics claim:

"Not only do we not have the originals [of the biblical manuscripts], we don't have the first copies of the originals.... What we have are copies made later—much later."[33]

■ What history actually tells us:

Although the original manuscripts from the biblical authors *have* been lost–probably forever–the copies that we possess today reliably reflect the inspired message of the original authors. Ancient people saw no reason to revere original manuscripts from important people, and—once documents became too worn to read easily—they did not retain the original manuscripts.[34] Instead, they made reliable copies and burned or buried the originals. Occasionally, the ink was scraped from the original, and the parchment was reused.

Despite the critics' claims, it *is* possible that we possess first-generation copies of the original New Testament manuscripts. In AD 200, churches in Corinth, Philippi, Thessalonica, Ephesus, and Rome still possessed original manuscripts from the apostolic authors.[35] Many portions of the New Testament that were copied between AD 100 and 200 have been found in Egypt; it is entirely possible that scribes copied at least a few of these documents from the original manuscripts.

What matters most, however, is not the *age* of the existing manuscripts but their *reliability*. When the manuscripts are compared, they completely agree with one another more than 99% of the time. Of the differences that remain, *not even one difference* decisively affects any aspect of Christian faith.

A Final Word

So will there be more sensational new findings about the Gospels—findings that supposedly demonstrate that these writings don't contain the gospel truth after all? Of course! The Holy Bible has withstood thousands of attempts to destroy its truth and to discredit its authority, and yet no one has succeeded. The truth and the authority of the Scriptures stand strong, regardless of every attempt to render them ineffective. So can the Bible be trusted? In a word, *yes*.

Author: Timothy Paul Jones, Ed.D
Excerpted material © 2007 Dr. Timothy Paul Jones. Excerpted from the book *Misquoting Truth: A Guide to the Fallacies of Bart Ehrman's Misquoting Jesus*. Published by InterVarsity Press (www.ivpress.com). All rights reserved. Reprinted by permission.
Visit the author on the Internet at: www.TimothyPaulJones.com
Special thanks to Alfred J. Hoerth, Director of Archaeology, Emeritus, Wheaton College; Lew Whallon.

Endnotes

1   Representative selections from Bart Ehrman, *Misquoting Jesus: The Story Behind Who Changed the Bible and Why* (New York: HarperCollins, 2005) 7, 10-11, 57. Hereafter, *Misquoting Jesus* will be cited as *MJ*, followed by the page numbers.

2   Bart Ehrman, *Jesus, Apocalyptic Prophet of the New Millennium* (New York: Oxford University, 1999) *JApP* 44-45. Hereafter, *Jesus, Apocalyptic Prophet of the New Millennium* will be cited as *JApP*, followed by the page numbers.

3   R. Bauckham, *Jesus and the Eyewitnesses: The Gospels as Eyewitness Testimony* (Grand Rapids, MI: William B. Eerdmans, 2006) 8-9, 20, 252-289.

4   Eusebius of Caesarea, *Historia Ecclesiastica*, 3:39; 5:8, 20; Bauckham, 14, 295-296; M. Hengel, *The Four Gospels and the One Gospel of Jesus Christ*, trans. John Bowden (Harrisburg, PA: Trinity Press, 2000) 36; C.-J. Thornton, *Der Zeuge des Zeugen: Lukas als Historiker der Paulusreisen*, ed. M. Hengel *WUNT* 56 (Tubingen, Germany: J.C.B. Mohr/Paul Siebeck, 1991) 10-82.

5   *JApP* 47-52.

6   For survey of orality in rabbinic and early Christian practice, see A. Millard, *Reading and Writing in the Time of Jesus* (New York: New York University Press, 2000), 188-192; R. Stein, *The Method and Message of Jesus' Teachings* rev. ed. (Louisville, KY: Westminster John Knox, 1994) 27-32; J. Harvey, *Listening to the Text: Oral Patterning in Paul's Letters* (Grand Rapids: Baker, 1998).

7   J.D.G. Dunn, *Jesus Remembered* (Grand Rapids, MI: William B. Eerdmans, 2003) 192-254; B. Witherington III, *The Jesus Quest* (Downers Grove, IL: InterVarsity Press, 1995) 80; see also J. Vansina, *Oral Tradition as History* (Madison, WI: University of Wisconsin, 1985) 15, 190-195.

8   Bart Ehrman, *Peter, Paul, and Mary Magdalene: The Followers of Jesus in History and Legend* (New York: Oxford University, 2006) 259. Hereafter, *Peter, Paul, and Mary Magdalene: The Followers of Jesus in History and Legend* will be cited as *PPM*, followed by the page numbers.

9   K. MacGregor, "1 Corinthians 15:3b—6a, 7 and the Bodily Resurrection of Jesus," in *Journal of the Evangelical Theological Society* 49 (June 2006): 225-234.

10 N.T. Wright, *The Resurrection of the Son of God* (Philadelphia, PA: Fortress, 2003) 318-319.

11 The repeated word-pattern which "and that" apparently translates is the distinctly Semitic *vav* consecutive. See P. Lapide, *The Resurrection of Jesus: A Jewish Perspective* (Minneapolis, MN: Augsburg, 1983) 98-99; G. Fee, *The First Epistle to the Corinthians* (Grand Rapids, MI: Eerdmans, 1987); 719, 722-726.

12 G. Ludemann, *The Resurrection of Jesus* (London, UK: SCM, 1994) 38; R. Funk, et al., *The Acts of Jesus* (San Francisco, CA: Polebridge, 1998) 454.

13 H. Bloom, *Jesus and Yahweh* (New York: Riverhead, 2005) 19.

14 *JApP* 45.

15 Millard, 28-29. Some scholars have argued that the apostles were literate and that they would have carried *pinakes* and noted significant sayings of Jesus. It seems to me, however, that this assumes a higher rate of literacy in Galilee and Judea—especially among persons in trades such as fishing—than the available evidence can sustain. For discussion and references, see B. Gerhardsson, *The Origins of the Gospel Traditions* (London, UK: SCM, 1979) 68-161, and, S. Lieberman, *Hellenism in Jewish Palestine* (New York: JTS, 1962) 203.

16 The abundance of surviving Roman taxation receipts, written in Greek, clearly demonstrates this fact. The epigraphical evidence includes not only brief receipts that follow simple formulas—for examples, see the numerous pieces of Elephantine and Egyptian ostraca in U. Wilken, *Griechische Ostraka aus Aegypten und Nubien* (Manchester, NH: Ayer, 1979) and in F. Preisigke, et al., *Sammelbuch griechischer Urkunden aus Aegypten* (Berlin: Walter de Gruyter, 1974)—but also more lengthy and complex receipts on papyrus, such as *POxy* 51:3609.

17 Millard, 31, 170. See the taxation documentation from the pre-Christian era and from the first and second centuries AD found in the Oxyrhynchus papyri *POxy* 49:3461; *POxy* 62:4334; *POxy* 24:2413; *POxy* 45:3241; and, *POxy* 66:4527, as well as more extensive contractual agreements such as the third-century *POxy* 43:3092.

18 J. Huskinson, *Experiencing Rome: Culture, Identity, and Power in the*

Roman Empire (London, UK: Routledge, 2000) 179-180; Nutton, 263-264. For a few of the many documentary examples of literacy among ancient physicians, see *P.Mich* 758; *POxy* 44:3195; *POxy* 45:3245; *POxy* 54:3729; *POxy* 63:4366; *POxy* 63:4370; *POxy* 64:4441; *POxy* 66:4529.

19 Millard, 176-185; R. Cribbiore, *Writing, Teachers, and Students in Graeco-Roman Egypt* (Atlanta, GA: Scholars, 1996) 1-5.

20 Ehrman seems to view the fact that a scribe wrote on Paul's behalf as being problematic for persons who embrace the Bible as divine truth (*MJ* 59), but Paul's use of a scribe does not preclude Paul's position as the source of the epistle. Certainly, he would have approved the letter before it was sent.

21 It is crucial to note that ancient persons were considered to be the writers of a document, even if they used a scribe to write the words. Notice how Paul declared, "I have written to you" in Romans 15:15, even though Tertius penned the actual document (see Romans 16:22). In the oral culture of the ancient Roman Empire, what scribes apparently recorded was the speaker-writer's oral performance of the document. This performance was then "re-performed" by the courier of the document. See J. Small, *Wax Tablets of the Mind: Cognitive Studies of Memory and Literacy in Classical Antiquity* (New York: Routledge, 1997) 160-201; Gregory Snyder, *Teachers and Texts in the Ancient World: Philosophers, Jews and Christians* (London, UK: Routledge, 2000) 191, 226-227; R. Thomas, *Literacy and Orality in Ancient Greece* (Cambridge, UK: Cambridge University Press, 2002) 36-40, 124-125.

22 Bart Ehrman, *Misquoting Jesus* expanded paperback edition (New York: HarperSanFrancisco, 2007) 254.

23 Gleason Archer, *A Survey of Old Testament Introduction* (Chicago, IL: Moody Press, 1994) 29.

24 *MJ* 7, 10-11.

25 D. Wallace, "The Gospel According to Bart," in *Journal of the Evangelical Theological Society* 49 (June 2006): 330.

26 *MJ* 149.

27 Bruce Metzger and Bart Ehrman, *The Text of the New Testament: Its Transmission, Corruption, and Restoration* (New York: Oxford University Press, 2005), 288-290.

28 Though I agree with Ehrman that "Junia" was a woman, the case is—in all fairness—not quite as clear-cut as Ehrman presents it. For an alternative viewpoint, see D. Wallace, "Junia among the Apostles": Retrieved December 1, 2006, from http://www.bible.org/page.php?page_id=1163/.

29 *MJ* dust jacket.

30 Bart Ehrman, *Lost Christianities* (New York: Oxford University Press, 2003) 54, 230.

31 Ehrman places the emergence of this principle later and summarizes it in this way: Authoritative texts had to be "ancient" (from the time of Jesus) and "apostolic" (from the first followers of Jesus or their associates) (*LC* 242-243). As Ehrman notes, two other standards came into play later in addition to antiquity and apostolicity; these two additional standards were *catholicity* (widespread usage among Christians) and *orthodoxy* (agreement with other Scriptures). For the earliest Christians, the three categories of *orthodoxy*, *apostolicity*, and *antiquity* do not seem to have been distinguished; all three categories were rooted in the assumption that eyewitness testimony was authoritative.

32 *MJ* 153.

33 *MJ* 7, 11.

34 Millard, 20, 33-34.

35 "Age iam, qui uoles curiositatem melius exercere in negotio salutis tuae, percurre ecclesias apostolicas apud quas ipsae adhuc cathedrae apostolorum suis locis praesident, apud quas ipsae *authenticae litterae* eorum recitantur sonantes uocem et repraesentantes faciem uniuscuiusque" (Tertullian of Carthage, *De Praescriptione Haereticorum*, 36:1: Retrieved November 4, 2006, from http://www.tertullian.org/).

36 *To the Ephesians* 10:2; 14:2; 18:1; 20:2; *To the Magnesians* 5:1; *To the Trallians* 1:3; 12:3; *To the Romans* 2:1-2; 6:1; *To the Smyrnans* 3:1-2; 6:1; *To Polycarp* 1:2; 2:2; 5:1.

37 F.F. Bruce, *The New Testament Documents: Are they Reliable?* (Downers Grove, IL: Inter Varsity, 1972) 20.

100 Prophecies
Fulfilled
by Jesus

Old Testament Prophecies
and New Testament Fulfillment

Color Coded by Date of Prophecy

COLOR KEY

Prophecies more than 1200 years before Jesus' birth are highlighted in green.

Prophecies more than 800 years before Jesus' birth are highlighted in tan

Prophecies more than 500 years before Jesus' birth are highlighted in blue

Prophecy	Old Testament References	New Testament Fulfillment
JESUS' BIRTH		
Be of the offspring of the woman, shall bruise the serpent's head	Genesis 3:14, 15 So the LORD God said to the serpent ..."And I will put enmity between you and the woman, and between your offspring and hers; he will crush your head, and you will strike his heel."	**Galatians 4:4** But when the time had fully come, God sent his Son, born of a woman, born under law, **Hebrews 2:14** Since the children have flesh and blood, he too shared in their humanity so that by his death he might destroy him who holds the power of death ... that is, the devil. **I John 3:8** He who does what is sinful is of the devil, because the devil has been sinning from the beginning. The reason the Son of God appeared was to destroy the devil's work.
All nations shall be blessed through Abraham	**Genesis 18:17, 18** Then the LORD said ... "Abraham will surely become a great and powerful nation, and all nations on earth will be blessed through him." Also Genesis 12:3; 22:18; 26:4; 28:14	**Acts 3:25, 26** "... He said to Abraham, 'Through your offspring all peoples on earth will be blessed.' When God raised up his servant, he sent him first to you to bless you ...' Also Matthew 1:1, 17; Galatians 3:16
Be of the tribe of Judah	**Genesis 49:8-10** "Judah, your brothers will praise you ... The sceptre will not depart from Judah, nor the ruler's staff from between his feet, until he comes to whom it belongs and the obedience of the nations is his." **Micah 5:2** "But you, Bethlehem Ephratah, though you are small among the clans of Judah, out of you will come for me one who will be ruler over Israel, whose origins are from of old, from ancient times."	**Matthew 1:1-3** A record of the genealogy of Jesus Christ the son of David, the son of Abraham ... Jacob the father of Judah and his brothers, Judah the father of Perez and Zerah ... **Hebrews 7:14** For it is clear that our Lord descended from Judah ... **Revelation 5:5** Then one of the elders said to me, "Do not weep! See, the Lion of the tribe of Judah, the Root of David, has triumphed. He is able to open the scroll and its seven seals."

Prophecy	Old Testament References	New Testament Fulfillment
Be born in the town of Bethlehem of Judea (Judah)	**Micah 5:2-5** "But you, Bethlehem Ephratah, though you are small among the clans of Judah, out of you will come for me one who will be ruler over Israel, whose origins are from of old, from ancient times." . . .	**Matthew 2:1-6** After Jesus was born in Bethlehem in Judea, during the time of King Herod, Magi from the east came to Jerusalem and asked, "Where is the one who has been born king of the Jews? . . ."
Be born a king of the line of David	**Isaiah 9:7** . . . He will reign on David's throne and over his kingdom . . . Also 2 Samuel 7:12, 13; Jeremiah 23:5; 30:9	**Matthew 1:1** A record of the genealogy of Jesus Christ the son of David, the son of Abraham . . . Also Luke 1:32; Acts 13:22, 23
A child to be born	**Isaiah 9:6** For to us a child is born . . . he will be called Wonderful Counselor, Mighty God . . .	**Luke 2:11** Today in the town of David a Saviour has been born to you; he is Christ the Lord.
Be born of a virgin	**Isaiah 7:13, 14** Then Isaiah said, "Hear now, you house of David! Is it not enough to try the patience of men? Will you try the patience of my God also? Therefore the Lord himself will give you a sign: The virgin will be with child and will give birth to a son, and will call him Immanuel (God with us)."	**Matthew 1:18-23** . . . His mother Mary was pledged to be married to Joseph, but before they came together, she was found to be with child through the Holy Spirit. **Luke 1:26-35** . . . God sent the angel . . . to a virgin pledged to be married to a man named Joseph, a descendant of David. The virgin's name was Mary. . . .
Kings shall bring him gifts, fall down before him	**Psalm 72:10, 11** The kings of Tarshish and of distant shores will bring tribute to him; the kings of Sheba and Seba will present him gifts. All kings will bow down to him and all nations will serve him.	**Matthew 2:1-11** After Jesus was born in Bethlehem in Judea, during the time of King Herod, Magi from the east came to Jerusalem . . . On coming to the house, they saw the child with his mother Mary, and they bowed down and worshipped him. Then they opened their treasures and presented him with gifts of gold and of incense and of myrrh.

Prophecy	Old Testament References	New Testament Fulfillment
Be born of the seed of Abraham	Genesis 17:7, 8; 26:3, 4	Matthew 1:1, 17; Galatians 3:16, 29; Hebrews 2:16
Be born of the seed of Isaac	Genesis 17:19; 21:12; 26:2-4	Matthew 1:2, 17; Romans 9:7; Hebrews 11:17-19
Be of the seed of Jacob; a star out of Jacob	Genesis 28:13, 14; Numbers 24:17, 19	Matthew 1:2; Luke 1:33; 3:23-38
Be a firstborn son, sanctified	Exodus 13:2; Numbers 3:13; 8:17	Luke 2:7, 23
Be a rod out of the stem of Jesse	Isaiah 11:1, 2	Matthew 1:6; Acts 13:22, 23
Massacre of children	Jeremiah 31:15	Matthew 2:16-18
Have eternal existence	Micah 5:2	John 1:1, 4; 8:58; Colossians 1:15-19

JESUS' LIFE AND MINISTRY

Be called out of Egypt	**Hosea 11:1** "When Israel was a child, I loved him, and out of Egypt I called my son...."	**Matthew 2:13-15, 19-21** ... So he ... took the child and his mother during the night and left for Egypt ...
Be rejected by his brethren	**Psalm 69:8** I am a stranger to my brothers, an alien to my own mother's sons ...	**John 7:3-5** Jesus' brothers said to him, "You ought to leave here ... so that your disciples may see the miracles you do...." For even his own brothers did not believe in him.
Rulers take council against him	**Psalm 2:1, 2** Why do the nations conspire and the peoples plot in vain? The kings of the earth take their stand and the rulers gather together against the LORD and against his Anointed One.	**Matthew 12:14** But the Pharisees went out and plotted how they might kill Jesus. **Matthew 26:3, 4** Then the chief priests and the elders ... plotted to arrest Jesus in some sly way and kill him. **Matthew 26:47** ... Judas ... arrived. With him was a large crowd armed with swords and clubs, sent from the chief priests and the elders of the people. See also Luke 23:11, 12

Prophecy	Old Testament References	New Testament Fulfillment
Be rejected as capstone	**Psalm 118:22, 23** The stone the builders rejected has become the capstone; the LORD has done this, and it is marvellous in our eyes.	**Matthew 21:42** Jesus said to them, "Have you never read in the Scriptures: "'The stone the builders rejected has become the capstone …
Was to enter the Temple	**Malachi 3:1** "…Then suddenly the Lord you are seeking will come to his temple; the messenger of the covenant, whom you desire, will come …" Also Haggai 2:7, 9	**Matthew 21:12-16** Jesus entered the temple area and drove out all who were buying and selling there…. See also Mark 11:11; Luke 2:25-47; Luke 19:45-47
Call those who were not his people	**Isaiah 55:4, 5** …Surely you will summon nations you know not, and nations that do not know you will hasten to you … Also Hosea 2:23	**Romans 9:23-26** …even us, whom he also called, not only from the Jews but also from the Gentiles? …
The King comes to Jerusalem riding on a donkey	**Zechariah 9:9** …See, your king comes to you, righteous and having salvation, gentle and riding on a donkey, on a colt, the foal of a donkey.	**Mark 11:1-10** …When they brought the colt to Jesus and threw their cloaks over it, he sat on it…. Also Matthew 21:1-5; Luke 19:28-38; John 12:14, 15
Be a "stone of stumbling" to the Jews	**Isaiah 8:14** …and he will be a sanctuary; but for both houses of Israel he will be a stone that causes men to stumble and a rock that makes them fall. And for the people of Jerusalem he will be a trap and a snare.	**Romans 9:31-33** …Israel …stumbled over the "stumbling-stone." As it is written: "See, I lay in Zion a stone that causes men to stumble and a rock that makes them fall, and the one who trusts in him will never be put to shame." **1 Peter 2:7, 8** …They stumble because they disobey the message—which is also what they were destined for.

Prophecy	Old Testament References	New Testament Fulfillment
Upon his coming, the deaf hear, the blind see	**Isaiah 29:18** In that day the deaf will hear the words of the scroll, and out of gloom and darkness the eyes of the blind will see. **Isaiah 35:5** Then will the eyes of the blind be opened and the ears of the deaf unstopped.	**Matthew 11:5** The blind receive sight, the lame walk, those who have leprosy are cured, the deaf hear, the dead are raised, and the good news is preached to the poor. Also John 9:39; Luke 7:19-22; Mark 7:37
Fulfill promises to Jews, be a light to the Gentiles	**Isaiah 42:6** "...I will keep you and will make you to be a covenant for the people and a light for the Gentiles..." **Isaiah 49:6** "...I will also make you a light for the Gentiles, that you may bring my salvation to the ends of the earth."	**Luke 2:25-32** "...a light for revelation to the Gentiles and for glory to your people Israel." **Acts 26:23** "...that the Christ would suffer and, as the first to rise from the dead, would proclaim light to his own people and to the Gentiles."
A new everlasting covenant	**Jeremiah 31:31-34** "...I will make a new covenant with the house of Israel and with the house of Judah. It will not be like the covenant I made with their forefathers...I will put my law in their minds and write it on their hearts...." Also Jeremiah 32:37-40; 50:5	**Luke 22:15-20** ..."This cup is the new covenant in my blood..." **Hebrews 10:15-20** ... "This is the covenant I will make with them after that time..." a new and living way opened for us ... Also Matthew 26:27-29; Mark 14:22-24; Luke 22:15-20; I Corinthians 11:25; Hebrews 8:8-12
Be a prophet like Moses, speaking God's words	Deuteronomy 18:15, 18, 19	Matthew 21:11; Luke 7:16; 24:19; John 6:14; 7:40; Acts 3:18-22
Be hated without reason	Psalm 35:19; 69:4	John 15:24, 25
Come to do the will of God	Psalm 40:7, 8	Matthew 26:39; Hebrews 10:5-9
Anointed by God	Psalm 45:6, 7	Hebrews 1:8, 9
Have great zeal for God's house	Psalm 69:9	John 2:17

Prophecy	Old Testament References	New Testament Fulfillment
Care for the poor and needy	Psalm 72:12-14	Luke 7:22
Speak in parables with hidden meaning	Psalm 78:2	Matthew 13:10-16; 34, 35 Luke 8:10
Will pray for His enemies	Psalm 109:4	Matthew 5:44; Luke 23:34
Be a priest after the order of Melchizedek	Psalm 110:4	Hebrews 5:1-6; 6:20; 7:15-17
People's hearts are hardened	Isaiah 6:9, 10	Matthew 13:13-15; John 12:37-40; Acts 28:24-27
His ministry in Zebulun, Naphtali, and Galilee	Isaiah 9:1, 2	Matthew 4:12-16
The government is on his shoulders	Isaiah 9:6	Matthew 28:18; 1 Corinthians 15:24, 25
Someone will prepare for the coming of the Lord	Isaiah 40:3-5	Matthew 3:3; Mark 1:3; Luke 3:3-5; John 1:23
The Spirit of the Lord rests upon him	Isaiah 11:2; 42:1; 61:1, 2	Matthew 3:16; Mark 1:10; Luke 3:22; 4:18; John 1:32; 3:34; Acts 10:38
Be a healer and savior, do miracles	Isaiah 35:4-6	Matthew 9:30; 11:4-6; 12:22; 20:34; 21:14; Mark 7:32-35; John 9:1-7; 11:47
Be a Shepherd who tends his sheep	Isaiah 40:10, 11	John 10:11; Hebrews 13:20; 1 Peter 2:25
Be a Servant of God	Isaiah 42:1-4	Matthew 12:16-21
The Redeemer to come out of Zion	Isaiah 59:16-20	Romans 11:26, 27
Nations shall walk in the light of the Lord	Isaiah 60:1-3	Matthew 4:16; Luke 2:32; John 12:46
Anointed to preach liberty to the captives	Isaiah 61:1-2a	Luke 4:16-21; Acts 10:38
His Spirit poured out upon people	Joel 2:28-32	Acts 2:16-23

Prophecy	Old Testament References	New Testament Fulfillment
David's house shall be restored	Amos 9:11, 12	Acts 15:16-18
God shall dwell among His people	Zechariah 2:10-13	John 1:14; Revelation 21:3
A new priesthood established	Zechariah 3:8	I Peter 2:5, 9; Revelation 1:6, 5:10
Messenger sent to prepare the way before Him	Malachi 3:1	Matthew 11:10; Mark 1:2-4, 7; Luke 7:27, 28
Prophet sent before the day of the Lord	Malachi 4:5, 6	Matthew 11:13, 14; Mark 9:11-13; Luke 1:17; 7:27, 28

JESUS' DEATH AND RESURRECTION

Prophecy	Old Testament References	New Testament Fulfillment
Be Passover sacrifice with no bone broken	**Exodus 12:46** It must be eaten inside one house; take none of the meat outside the house. Do not break any of the bones. **Numbers 9:12** They must not leave any of it till morning or break any of its bones. When they celebrate the Passover, they must follow all the regulations. Also Psalm 34:20	**John 19:31-36** . . . But when they came to Jesus and found that he was already dead, they did not break his legs. . . . These things happened so that the scripture would be fulfilled: "Not one of his bones will be broken."
Be hung upon a tree as a curse for us	**Deuteronomy 21:23** . . . Be sure to bury him that same day, because anyone who is hung on a tree is under God's curse. You must not desecrate the land the LORD your God is giving you as an inheritance.	**Galatians 3:13** Christ redeemed us from the curse of the law by becoming a curse for us, for it is written: "Cursed is everyone who is hung on a tree."
Be thirsty during his execution	**Psalm 22:15** My strength is dried up like a potsherd, and my tongue sticks to the roof of my mouth; you lay me in the dust of death.	**John 19:28** Later, knowing that all was now completed, and so that the Scripture would be fulfilled, Jesus said, "I am thirsty."

Prophecy	Old Testament References	New Testament Fulfillment
Be accused by false witnesses	**Psalm 27:12** Do not hand me over to the desire of my foes, for false witnesses rise up against me, breathing out violence. **Psalm 35:11** Ruthless witnesses come forward; they question me on things I know nothing about.	**Matthew 26:60** . . . many false witnesses came forward. . . . **Mark 14:55-61** . . . Then some stood up and gave this false testimony against him. . . .
Be struck on the head	**Micah 5:1** . . . They will strike Israel's ruler on the cheek with a rod.	**Matthew 27:30** They spat on him, and took the staff and struck him on the head again and again.
Have hands and feet pierced	**Psalm 22:16** Dogs have surrounded me; a band of evil men has encircled me, they have pierced my hands and my feet. **Zechariah 12:10** ". . . They will look on me, the one they have pierced, and they will mourn for him as . . . for a firstborn son.	**Matthew 27:35** . . . they had crucified him . . . Also John 19:18, 34-37 **John 20:25-29** . . . "Unless I see the nail marks in his hands . . . and put my hand into his side, I will not believe it." . . . Then he said ". . . Reach out your hand and put it into my side." . . .
Have soldiers cast lots for his coat	**Psalm 22:18** They divide my garments among them and cast lots for my clothing.	**John 19:23, 24** . . . This garment was seamless . . . "Let's not tear it," they said to one another. "Let's decide by lot who will get it." Also Matthew 27:35; Mark 15:24; Luke 23:34
Be given gall and vinegar (sour wine)	**Psalm 69:20-22** . . . They put gall in my food and gave me vinegar for my thirst. . . .	**Matthew 27:34** There they offered Jesus wine to drink, mixed with gall; but after tasting it, he refused to drink it. Also Matthew 27:48; Mark 15:23; 15:36; Luke 23:36; John 19:29

Prophecy	Old Testament References	New Testament Fulfillment
Be beaten and spat upon	**Isaiah 50:6** I offered my back to those who beat me, my cheeks to those who pulled out my beard; I did not hide my face from mocking and spitting.	**Matthew 26:67** Then they spat in his face and struck him with their fists. Others slapped him. **Matthew 27:26-30** ... They spat on him, and took the staff and struck him on the head again and again. Also Mark 14:65; 15:15-19; Luke 22:63-65; John 19:1
Be betrayed by a friend	**Psalm 41:9** Even my close friend, whom I trusted, he who shared my bread, has lifted up his heel against me. **Psalm 55:12-14** If an enemy were insulting me, I could endure it; if a foe were raising himself against me, I could hide from him. But it is you, a man like myself, my companion, my close friend, with whom I once enjoyed sweet fellowship as we walked with the throng at the house of God.	**Matthew 26:14-16** Then one of the Twelve ... the one called Judas Iscariot ... went to the chief priests and asked, "What are you willing to give me if I hand him over to you?" ... **Matthew 26:23** Jesus replied, "The one who has dipped his hand into the bowl with me will betray me." Also Matthew 26:47-50; Luke 22:19-23, 48; John 13:18-30; 18:2-5
Be despised and rejected	**Isaiah 53:2, 3** ... He was despised and rejected by men, ... Like one from whom men hide their faces he was despised, and we esteemed him not.	**Luke 17:25** But first he must suffer many things and be rejected by this generation. **Luke 23:18** ... "Away with this man! Release Barabbas to us!" Also Matthew 26:67; John 1:11
Be accused and afflicted, but did not open his mouth	**Isaiah 53:7** He was oppressed and afflicted, yet he did not open his mouth; he was led like a lamb to the slaughter, and as a sheep before her shearers is silent, so he did not open his mouth.	**Matthew 27:12** When he was accused by the chief priests and the elders, he gave no answer. **Luke 23:9** He plied him with many questions, but Jesus gave him no answer. Also Matthew 26:62, 63; 27:14; Mark 14:61; 15:5; John 19:9

Prophecy	Old Testament References	New Testament Fulfillment
Commit his spirit into God's hand	**Psalm 31:5** Into your hands I commit my spirit; redeem me, O Lord, the God of truth.	**Luke 23:46** Jesus called out with a loud voice, "Father, into your hands I commit my spirit." When he had said this, he breathed his last.
Be buried with the rich	**Isaiah 53:9** He was assigned a grave with the wicked, and with the rich in his death, though he had done no violence, nor was any deceit in his mouth.	**Matthew 27:57-60** ... there came a rich man from Arimathea, named Joseph, who had himself become a disciple of Jesus.... he asked for Jesus' body, ... and placed it in his own new tomb....
Be numbered (crucified) with transgressors	**Isaiah 53:12** ... he poured out his life unto death, and was numbered with the transgressors ...	**Matthew 27:38** Two robbers were crucified with him, ... Also Mark 15:27, 28; Luke 22:37; 23:32, 33
The 30 pieces of silver buy the potter's field	**Zechariah 11:12, 13** ... So they paid me thirty pieces of silver.... I took the thirty pieces of silver and threw them into the house of the Lord to the potter.	**Matthew 27:3, 6-10** ... Judas ... returned the thirty silver coins to the chief priests and the elders ... they decided to use the money to buy the potter's field ...
Be sold for thirty pieces of silver	Zechariah 11:12	Matthew 26:14, 15
Be Passover male lamb, without blemish, slain, with blood applied as protection from judgment	Exodus 12:1-11, Isaiah 53:7	John 1:29-36; 1 Corinthians 5:7, 8; 1 Peter 1:18, 19; Revelation 5:6-13; 7:14; 21:22-27; 22:1-4
Be lifted up, just as Moses lifted up a serpent	Numbers 21:8, 9	John 3:14, 15
Be raised from the dead	Psalm16:8-11	Luke 24:6-8; John 20; Acts 1:3; 2:32; 13:34-37; 2 Timothy 2:8
Conquer death through his resurrection	Psalm 16:8-11; 49:15; 86:13	Acts 2:24-36; 13:30-39; 1 Corinthians 15:3, 4
Feel forsaken by God	Psalm 22:1	Matthew 27:46; Mark 15:34
Be mocked and insulted by many	Psalm 22:7, 8, 17	Matthew 27:31, 39-43; Mark 15:29-32; Luke 23:35-39
Friends stand afar off	Psalm 38:11; 88:18	Matthew 26:56-58; 27:55; Mark 15:40; Luke 23:49
Ascend on high	Psalm 68:18	Luke 24:51; Acts 1:9; Ephesians 4:8
Reproaches of others fall on him	Psalm 69:9	Romans 15:3

Prophecy	Old Testament References	New Testament Fulfillment
Another to succeed Judas	Psalm 109:7, 8	Acts 1:16-20
Be a Son who is given	Isaiah 9:6	John 3:16; Romans 8:32
Swallow up death in victory	Isaiah 25:8	1 Corinthians 15:54-57
Be mistreated, hardly recognized	Isaiah 52:14	Hebrews 5:8; 1 Peter 2:21
Bare our griefs and carry our sorrows	Isaiah 53:4, 5	Matthew 8:17; Romans 5:6-8
Be wounded for our transgressions	Isaiah 53:5	1 Corinthians 15:3; 2 Corinthians 5:21; 1 Peter 3:18
Be led as a lamb to the slaughter	Isaiah 53:7	John 1:29, 36; Acts 8:28-35; 1 Peter 1:19; Revelation 5:6
Be sinless and without guile	Isaiah 53:9	1 Peter 2:22
Make intercession for the transgressors	Isaiah 53:12	Luke 23:34; "Father, forgive them for they know not what they do."
Be made into an offering for sin	Isaiah 53:10, 11	Acts 10:43; 13:38, 39; Romans 3:21-26; 4:5-8; Ephesians 1:7; 1 Peter 2:21-25; 1 John 2:2
Be "cut off" at a specific time after Jerusalem wall is rebuilt, before the Temple is destroyed	Daniel 9:24-26; Zechariah 9:9	Matthew 21:1-5; 1:15; 24:1, 2 Luke 19:37, 38; John 12:13-15
His body would be pierced	Zechariah 12:10	John 19:34-37
Shepherd smitten, sheep scattered (deserted by his followers)	Zechariah 13:6, 7	Matthew 26:31, 56; Mark 14:27; John 16:32

JESUS' TITLES AND ATTRIBUTES

Prophecy	Old Testament References	New Testament Fulfillment
"I Am" (Jehovah)	Exodus 3:13-15	John 8:24; 13:19
A Prophet like Moses	Deuteronomy 18:18, 19	John 1:21; 6:14; Acts 3:22, 23; Hebrews 3:1-6

Prophecy	Old Testament References	New Testament Fulfillment
The throne of David established forever	2 Samuel 7:12, 13, 16, 25, 26; Psalm 89:3, 4, 36, 37; Isaiah 9:7 1 Chronicles 17:11-14, 23-27;	Luke 1:32, 33; Acts 2:29-36; 2 Timothy 2:8; Hebrews 1:8
The promised Redeemer	Job 19:25-27; Psalm 130:7, 8; Isaiah 59:20	Galatians 4:4, 5; Titus 2:13, 14
The Son of God	Psalm 2:7	Matthew 3:17; 8:29; 16:16; Mark 1:11; Luke 1:32, 35; Acts 13:33; Hebrews 1:5; 5:5; 2 Peter 1:17
Delights to do God's will	Psalm 40:8	John 4:34; 6:38
A King known for righteousness, anointed	Psalm 45:1-7	Hebrews 1:8, 9
Seed of David	Psalm 89:3, 4	John 7:42; Acts 13:22, 23
The firstborn over all creation	Psalm 89:27	Romans 8:29; Colossians 1:15
Never changing, everlasting	Psalm 102:24-27	Hebrews 1:10-12; 13:8
David's son; David's Lord at God's right hand	Psalm 110:1	Matthew 22:41-45; Mark 12:35-37; 16:19; Acts 7:56; Romans 1:3; Ephesians 1:20; Hebrews 1:3
A Priest according to the order of Melchizedek	Psalm 110:4	Hebrews 5:5, 6, 10; 6:20; 7:1-22
The Chief Cornerstone	Psalm 118:22, 23	Matthew 21:42; Mark 12:10, 11; Luke 20:17; Acts 4:10-12; Ephesians 2:20; 1 Peter 2:4-7
The way of repentance for all nations	Isaiah 2:2-4	Luke 24:47

Prophecy	Old Testament References	New Testament Fulfillment
Immanuel, God with us	Isaiah 7:14; 8:8, 10	Matthew 1:21-23; John 1:14; 14:8-11; Colossians 2:9
A stone of stumbling, a rock of offense	Isaiah 8:14, 15	Matthew 21:42-44; Romans 9:32, 33; 1 Peter 2:6-8
The light which has shone out of darkness	Isaiah 9:1, 2	Matthew 4:14-16; Luke 1:7, 9; 2:32; John 1:4, 5
Prince of Peace	Isaiah 9:6	John 14:27; Acts 10:36; Romans 5:1; Ephesians 2:14; Colossians 1:20
Full of wisdom, power and righteousness	Isaiah 11:1-10	Acts 10:38; 1 Corinthians 1:30; Ephesians 1:17; Colossians 2:2, 3
The key of the house of David is upon his shoulder	Isaiah 22:21-25	Revelation 3:7
The stone in Zion, a sure foundation	Isaiah 28:16	Romans 9:33; 1 Peter 2:6
God's elect Servant, in whom he delights	Isaiah 42:1-4	Matthew 12:17-21; Philippians 2:7
Spirit of the LORD shall rest on him	Isaiah 61:1	Matthew 3:16; Luke 4:18
The Righteous Branch	Jeremiah 23:5, 6; 33:15, 16	Romans 3:22; 1 Corinthians 1:30; 2 Corinthians 5:21; Philippians 3:9
The Good Shepherd	Ezekiel 34:23, 24; 37:24	John 10:11; Hebrews 13:20; 1 Peter 2:25
The enthroned High Priest	Zechariah 6:12, 13	Hebrews 7:11-28; 8:1, 2
Sun of Righteousness; the Dayspring; our Light	Malachi 4:2, 3	Luke 1:78; Ephesians 5:14; 2 Peter 1:19; John 8:12; Revelation 2:28; 22:16

This chart refers primarily to the prophecies fulfilled by the first coming of Jesus.
It does not contain all the prophecies that refer to Jesus' second coming.

The Gospels: "Lost" & Found

Why Are There Only Four Gospels?

Were Other "Gospels" Included in the New Testament, then Later Rejected?

How Do We Know the Gospels Are Reliable?

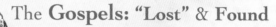

The Gospels: "Lost" & Found

The New Testament begins with four accounts of the life of Jesus Christ commonly known as "Gospels," a word that means "good news" or "victorious tidings." The Gospels According to Matthew, Mark, Luke, and John have been familiar to Christians for so many centuries that many believers have assumed these Gospels are the only retellings of the life of Jesus that ever existed. But there are more than a *dozen* other "Gospels," plus several supposed accounts of episodes from Jesus' life that aren't known by the name of "Gospel."

Some of these alternative "Gospels" have been familiar among scholars for centuries. Dan Brown's novel *The Da Vinci Code* popularized several "lost Gospels," including *Gospel of Philip*, *Gospel of Mary Magdalene*, and *Gospel of Thomas*. A couple of years later the *Gospel of Judas* was reconstructed and translated anew. The media implied that *Gospel of Judas* and other lost Gospels provide information about the historical Jesus that isn't included in the New Testament Gospels. Several writers and entertainment corporations were quick to turn a profit by sensationalizing the news of this reconstructed "Gospel." Indeed, the viewpoints found in the "lost Gospels" *do* differ from the New Testament Gospels.

According to New Testament Gospels	According to "Lost Gospels"
Jesus was fully human and fully divine	Jesus was a spirit who seemed human or a mere human uniquely inhabited by a divine spirit (Gnostic gospels)
Judas Iscariot willingly chose to betray Jesus	Jesus told Judas to betray him (*Gospel of Judas*)
The first miraculous sign that Jesus performed was turning water to wine at Cana	Jesus performed self-serving miracles throughout his childhood ("infancy Gospels")

How likely is it that the lost Gospels really tell us the truth about Jesus Christ? An open-minded look at the historical record quickly reveals that there is little reason to doubt the New Testament Gospels and great reason to reject the so-called "lost Gospels."

True or False?

What if the version of the life of Jesus that's found in the Bible isn't the right one? What if there were other accounts of his life and ministry? And what if none of these versions actually represents eyewitness testimony about Jesus? That's precisely what some scholars are teaching, not just on college campuses but in popular literature and on television.

Popular scholars such as Bart Ehrman and Elaine Pagels, whose books boast titles such as *The Gnostic Gospels*, *Lost Scriptures*, and *Lost Christianities*, make claims such as this one: "Many years passed before Christians agreed concerning which books should comprise their sacred scriptures. . . . In part this was because other books were available, also written by Christians, many of their authors claiming to be the original apostles of Jesus, yet advocating points of view quite different from those later embodied in the canon."[1]

Indeed, the viewpoints found in these writings, many of which are called "Gospels," *do* differ from the New Testament Gospels. In fact, many include descriptions of Jesus that directly contradict the Gospels according to Matthew, Mark, Luke, and John. Most significantly, the "lost Gospels" consistently depict the *nature of Jesus* in ways that disagree with the Gospels according to Matthew, Mark, Luke, and John. For example, the New Testament writings describe Jesus as fully divine and yet fully human (see, for example, Philippians 2:5-11). But, according to other writings, Jesus Christ was a spirit who merely *seemed* human. In others, such as *Gospel of Philip*, Jesus of Nazareth—a human being—was possessed by a Christ-spirit; then on the cross, this Christ-spirit abandoned the human Jesus.

(Courtesy of the Schøyen Collection, Oslo and London)

So what's at stake when it comes to the lost Gospels? Nothing less than the nature of Jesus Christ, the essence of Christian faith! Simply put, if the authors of the lost Gospels were telling the truth, the perspective on Jesus that's found in the New Testament Gospels is false. Let's look together at the historical evidence, though, and see what we actually find.

Earliest known fragment of *Acts of Paul*. When it was discovered that *Acts of Paul* was a fictional text, Christians rejected its authority.

■ What are the "lost Gospels"?

The term "lost Gospels" usually refers to ancient writings that were excluded from the New Testament, even though they included *supposed* recollections of events and teachings from the life of Jesus. A few of these "lost Gospels" have lasted throughout the centuries. Others survive only in tiny fragments of papyrus or in brief quotations found in the writings of early Christian scholars. Several "lost Gospels" were discovered anew in the past 100 years. Copies of some texts—such as *Gospel of Philip, Gospel of Thomas, Gospel of Truth,* and *Coptic Gospel of the Egyptians*— were unearthed in 1945 in Egypt, near a village known as Nag Hammadi.

Truth about the New Testament Gospels

■ Why were the "lost Gospels" excluded from the New Testament?

The lost Gospels were excluded because they did not include reliable, eyewitness testimony about Jesus. Some scholars today depict this decision as having been made by powerful church leaders in the fourth century, three centuries after the books in the New Testament were written. One such scholar claims that a letter from a powerful bishop, Athanasius of Alexandria, established the list of authoritative books in AD 367. He claims, "Athanasius wrote his annual pastoral letter to the Egyptian churches under his jurisdiction, and in it he included advice concerning which books should be read as Scripture in the churches. He lists our twenty-seven books, excluding all others. This is the first surviving instance of anyone affirming our set of books as the New Testament. And even Athanasius did not settle the matter. Debates continued for decades, even centuries."[2]

Each fact in this summary is *technically* correct, but it leaves out several key truths, leaving readers with false impressions—such as, (1) until the late fourth century, there was no consensus about which Christian writings were authoritative and true, and (2) even then the church's standard was simply the authoritative statement of a powerful bishop.

So when *did* Christians agree on which writings were authoritative in their congregations? And what was the standard for these decisions? Hints of this standard can be found in first-century Christian writings. The basic idea was something like this: *Testimony that could be connected to eyewitnesses of the risen Lord was uniquely authoritative among early Christians.*[3] It was *not* one specific person or a powerful group in the early church that decided to include certain books in the New Testament. *From the beginning, authoritative testimony about Jesus Christ had to have its source in eyewitnesses of the risen Lord.* The lost Gospels were excluded by the fact that they could not be clearly connected to persons who walked and talked with Jesus; therefore, their testimony could not be considered authoritative or reliable.

■ When did Christians begin to treat the words of eyewitnesses as the most reliable testimony about Jesus?

Even while the New Testament books were being written, the words of people who saw and followed the risen Lord—specifically, the words and writings of the apostles—carried special weight in the churches (see Acts 1:21-26; 15:6—16:5; 1 Corinthians 4—5; 9:1-12; Galatians 1:1-12; 1 Thessalonians 5:26-27). After the apostles' deaths, Christians continued to cherish the testimony of eyewitnesses and their associates. Around AD 110, Papias of Hierapolis put it this way: "So, if anyone who had served the elders came, I asked about their sayings in detail—what Andrew or Peter said, or what was said by Philip or Thomas or James or John or Matthew or any other of the Lord's followers."[4] The people most likely to know the truth about Jesus were the ones who had encountered Jesus personally or the close associates of these witnesses. So, although Christians wrangled for several centuries about *which* writings were authoritative, it was something much greater than political machinations that drove their decisions. Their goal was to determine which books could be clearly connected to eyewitnesses of the risen Lord.

■ Why did only four Gospels make it into the New Testament if so many Gospels were available to early Christians?

Only four Gospels—the ones known to us as the Gospels according to Matthew, Mark, Luke, and John—could be clearly connected to firsthand accounts of the risen Lord. Unlike the "lost Gospels," each of the New Testament Gospels was written in the first century AD, at a time when the eyewitnesses of Jesus' ministry were still alive. (The earthly ministry of Jesus began around AD 28 and lasted until AD 30 or so.) What's more, it's possible to trace widespread awareness among Christians that these Gospels represented eyewitness testimony back to the late first century, within a few years of the time when the last of the New Testament Gospels was written.

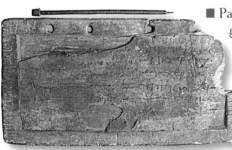

(Courtesy of the Schøyen Collection, Oslo and London)

Tax collectors were known to carry *pinakes*, books with wooden pages covered with wax. Notes were scratched into the wax using styluses.

■ Papias of Hierapolis—a church leader in the geographic area known today as Turkey, born about the time the Gospels were being written and a friend of Philip's four daughters mentioned in Acts 21:9[5]—received his information about the first two New Testament Gospels from the first generation of Christians. According to Papias, the primary source for Matthew's Gospel was the testimony of the Matthew, a follower of Jesus and former tax collector (Matthew 9:9).

This painting from the ruins of Pompeii depicts two methods for writing in the first century: The man holds a papyrus scroll while his wife holds a stylus and wax tablet.

■ Papias also wrote that the author of Mark's Gospel had served as Peter's translator when Peter preached in the early churches. As such, what Mark recorded in his Gospel was the witness of Peter himself.

■ About the same time as Papias recorded these recollections, a pastor named Polycarp of Smyrna referred to the words of the apostle Paul as "Scripture."

■ In a mid-second-century document known as the Muratorian Fragment, an unknown church leader reports that Luke's Gospel came from Luke, the apostle Paul's physician, and that this Gospel included eyewitness accounts from people that Luke interviewed.[6]

■ The Muratorian Fragment also makes it clear that the apostle John was the source for the Gospel that bears John's name.

■ Also in the mid-second-century, another church leader—Irenaeus of Lyons—reported that he had received these same traditions about the four Gospels from Christians of the first and second centuries.[7]

So, from the first century onward, it seems to have been widely recognized that the Gospels now known by the names of Matthew, Mark, Luke, and John represented eyewitness testimony about the life and ministry of Jesus Christ. In contrast, *none* of the "lost Gospels" can be connected to firsthand testimony.

■ How do we know that Matthew, Mark, Luke, and John were really the sources of the Gospels that bear their names?

Consistent and reliable traditions have connected the names of Matthew, Mark, Luke, and John with these Gospels from the first century onward. Some scholars claim that the New Testament Gospels received their names in the same way that some of the "lost Gospels" received their titles—people wanted these writings to seem authoritative; so, they simply added names of eyewitnesses, even though these people really didn't write the Gospels at all. For example, one scholar puts it this way: "Sometime in the second century, when [Christians] recognized the need for *apostolic* authorities, they attributed these books to apostles (Matthew and John) and close companions of apostles (Mark, the secretary of Peter; and Luke the traveling companion of Paul)."[8]

The first problem with this skeptical line of thinking is that the Gospels According to Matthew, Mark, Luke, and John seem to have been connected with their authors as soon as the Gospels began to circulate widely. At this time, some people who knew the authors would still have been alive; under these circumstances, it would have been difficult to ascribe false names to the Gospels without someone protesting.

But there's another problem with the skeptics' claims: By the end of the first century, the four New Testament Gospels had circulated thousands of miles throughout the Roman Empire. In fact, a fragment of John's Gospel from early years of the second century—a portion known as the John Rylands Papyrus or P52–has been found in Egypt, hundreds of miles from the Gospel's point of origin in Asia Minor! Without rapid communication and without centralized church leadership, what would have happened if second-century Christians began ascribing false, apostolic names to the Gospels that had already spread this far from their places of origin? Most likely, each church would have connected a different author with each Gospel. Churches in Asia Minor might have ascribed a Gospel to the apostle Andrew, for example, while churches in Judea might have connected the same Gospel with Thaddeus or James or Jude. But, *in every titled manuscript copy of the four New Testament Gospels, no matter what part of the world in which it was used, each Gospel is connected to the same author.*

■ How did early Christians determine which writings really came from eyewitnesses?

(Courtesy of CSNTM.org)

Gospel According to John, around the tenth century AD.

These decisions were informed by a combination of *oral history, external and internal evidence.*

■ **Oral history:** Most of the knowledge about the origins of the New Testament books probably passed orally from one generation to another. From the first century onward, the names of Matthew, Mark, Luke, and John were connected with the four New Testament Gospels, and the writings of early Christians such as Ignatius of Antioch suggest that it would have been widely known that Paul wrote the epistles attributed to him.

■ **External evidence:** When no clear tradition was available to connect a book to an eyewitness, church members might explore *external evidence* about a book's origins. For example, a generation after the deaths of the apostles, a church leader near Rome considered which Christian writings should be viewed as authoritative. His conclusions can be found in a document known today as "the Muratorian Fragment." After listing the books that he viewed as authoritative, here's what this leader said that he had discovered regarding a popular book known as *The Shepherd*: "Hermas composed *The Shepherd* quite recently—in our times, in the city of Rome, while his brother Pius served as overseer.... While it should indeed be read, it cannot be read publicly for the people of the church—it is counted neither among the prophets (for their number has been completed) nor among the apostles (for it is after their time)."[9] Notice the reasons: This writing could not be added to the Old Testament prophets because the time of the Hebrew prophets had passed, and—with the deaths of the apostles—the time of the apostolic eyewitnesses had also ended. This teacher didn't forbid believers to read *The Shepherd*; he simply pointed out that the book should not serve as an authoritative text.

■ **Internal evidence:** Other times, Christians might conclude on the basis of *internal evidence* that a certain book did not represent eyewitness testimony. For example, in AD 199, a leading pastor named Serapion was told that a certain Gospel was "inscribed with Peter's name."[10] Since it bore the name of an apostolic eyewitness, Serapion allowed the Gospel to be used in the churches. When Serapion read *Gospel of Peter* for himself, however, he recognized he'd made a mistake. Although *Gospel of Peter* didn't directly contradict the New Testament Gospels, certain phrases in the book could be taken to imply that Jesus wasn't fully human. What's more, Serapion probably knew from oral tradition that John Mark had once served as Peter's translator and that the Gospel According to Mark represented the words of Peter; yet, the *Gospel of Peter* added many fanciful details that never appeared in Mark's Gospel—like a towering, talking cross that accompanied the risen Jesus out of the tomb. After comparing *Gospel of Peter* to "the writings handed down to us"—that was Serapion's term for the New Testament texts that were connected indisputably to eyewitnesses—Serapion concluded that *Gospel of Peter* did *not* represent the eyewitness testimony of Simon Peter, and he reversed his previous decision. As it turns out, Serapion was correct: The language and thought-patterns in *Gospel of Peter* have convinced most scholars today that the book was written a generation after Simon Peter's death.[11]

■ Why do we call the chosen books of the New Testament a "canon"?

> *"We,* brothers and sisters, receive Peter and the rest of the apostles as we would receive Christ himself. But those writings that are falsely ascribed with their names, we carefully reject, knowing that no such writings have ever been handed down to us."
>
> —Serapion of Antioch, late second century AD[12]

The word "canon" comes from the Greek word *kanon,* which means "measuring stick," and these are the writings that "measure" Christians' faithfulness to Jesus Christ. It was not until the fourth century AD that the authoritative writings about Jesus Christ began to be known as a "canon." The idea of recognizing certain writings as authoritative, however, emerged much earlier, apparently in the first century. Each authoritative writing was expected to be connected to an eyewitness of the risen Lord, to be recognized in churches throughout the known world, and not to contradict other writings about Jesus. Although debates continued into the fourth century about a few writings—including the letters of Peter, John's second and third letters, and the letters of James and Jude—Christians universally agreed at least as early as the second century on the authority of at least nineteen of the books in the New Testament. From the beginning, Christians unanimously embraced at least the four Gospels, Acts, Paul's letters, and first epistle of John. (*See chart on page 13.*) Even if this handful of books had been the *only* documents that represented eyewitness testimony about Jesus, every vital truth of Christian faith would remain completely intact.

Truth about the "Lost Gospels"

■ Who wrote the "lost Gospels"?

No one knows for sure. Even though the names of Jesus' apostles and other companions are attached to several lost Gospels, no evidence exists to suggest that the authors of these texts even *could* have been eyewitnesses of the ministry of Jesus. In many cases, names such as "Mary" or "Philip" have been attached to these Gospels simply because these individuals are such prominent characters in the book. In a few cases—such as *Gospel of Thomas,* for example—the Gospel does actually claim to come from a prominent apostle or church leader, though it is clear from the language used in the book that the document was written long after the death of its namesake.

■ How are these writings different from the New Testament writings?

The "lost Gospels" were primarily fanciful accounts of Jesus' life, or they were written to promote a theology that contradicts the eyewitness testimony found in the New Testament. A few lost Gospels—for example, *Infancy Gospel of Thomas, Infancy Gospel of James,* and perhaps *Gospel of Peter*—seem to have been penned by well-meaning Christians who felt compelled to expand stories in the New Testament. Many parts of these writings don't directly contradict anything in the New Testament, but they tend to expand the New Testament accounts in fanciful and theologically problematic ways. For example, according to these writings, Jesus used his divine powers for his own benefit throughout his childhood. A couple of lost Gospels—such as *Gospel of the Lord* and *Gospel of the Ebionites*—were variations of the New Testament Gospels, edited to fit the theology of certain sects.

The distinct theology of most of the "lost Gospels" was, however, *Gnostic.* From the perspective of most Gnostics, the deity who created the universe was not the true or supreme God; the creator of the physical world was an evil deity, a rebel against a higher and greater deity. Since they understood the cosmos to be the product of an evil deity, most Gnostics viewed everything physical—especially the role of women in reproduction—as evil; they also claimed that Jesus Christ only *seemed* human. According to Gnostics, Christ came to deliver humanity from the limitations of the physical world. As such, Gnostics were not typically interested in the actual, historical events of the life of Jesus; the Gnostics focused most of their attention on other-worldly sayings and myths, many of which depicted biblical villains as heroes and vice-versa.

(Courtesy of the Schøyen Collection, Oslo and London)

Inkwell discovered near the site where the Dead Sea Scrolls were copied.

THE NEW TESTAMENT/ORTHODOX CHRISTIANITY ■	GNOSTIC ("SECRET") DOCUMENTS

AD50   AD100

28–30
Jesus' death
and resurrection.

49–96 The books of the New Testament are written.

■ How many lost Gospels are there?

If a Gospel is defined as an ancient retelling of the events and teachings of Jesus' life, there are fewer than thirty known Gospels. Most texts survive only in incomplete fragments. Here's a summary of many of the lost Gospels, most of which could not have been written by eyewitnesses:

■ *Gospel of Basilides (Gnostic writing, mid-second century AD)* Gnostic writing, now lost, mentioned by several early Christians.

■ *Gospel of the Ebionites (Ebionite writing, second century AD)* Surviving only in fragmented quotations in the writings of early Christians, *Gospel of the Ebionites* appears to have been a variation of *Gospel of the Hebrews*, edited to fit the theology of a sect known as "Ebionites." The Ebionites believed Jesus was a human being, adopted by God at his baptism.

"Matthew composed his Gospel among the Hebrews in their language, while Peter and Paul were preaching the Gospel in Rome and building up the church there. After their deaths, Mark—Peter's follower and interpreter—handed down to us Peter's proclamation in written form. Luke, the companion of Paul, wrote in a book the Gospel proclaimed by Paul. Finally, John—the Lord's own follower, the one who leaned against his chest—composed the Gospel while living in Ephesus, in Asia."

—Irenaeus of Lyons, mid- to late second century AD[13]

■ *Gospel, Egerton (Fragments from an ancient document, second century AD)* Not actually a Gospel but a few fragments from an unknown source, the "Egerton Gospel" includes four stories about Jesus. Three of these stories appear, in varying forms, in the New Testament Gospels (Mk. 1:40–45; 12:13–17; Jn. 5:39–47; 10:33–39).

■ *Gospel of the Egyptians (Ancient writing, perhaps Gnostic, second century AD)* Presented as a dialogue between Jesus and a female disciple named Salome, *Gospel of the Egyptians* encourages all believers to practice celibacy.

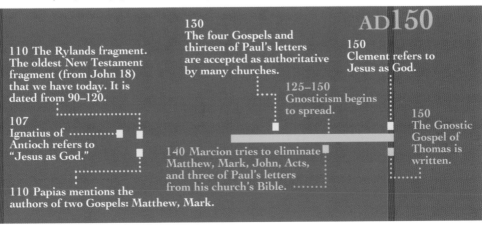

AD150

130
The four Gospels and thirteen of Paul's letters are accepted as authoritative by many churches.

150
Clement refers to Jesus as God.

110 The Rylands fragment. The oldest New Testament fragment (from John 18) that we have today. It is dated from 90–120.

125–150
Gnosticism begins to spread.

107
Ignatius of Antioch refers to "Jesus as God."

140 Marcion tries to eliminate Matthew, Mark, John, Acts, and three of Paul's letters from his church's Bible.

150
The Gnostic Gospel of Thomas is written.

110 Papias mentions the authors of two Gospels: Matthew, Mark.

■ *Coptic Gospel of the Egyptians* *(Gnostic writing, late third century AD)*
Coptic Gospel of the Egyptians recounts a Gnostic myth in which
Jesus is presented as a reincarnation of Seth, the third
son of Adam and Eve.

■ *Gospel of Eve* *(Gnostic writing, probably third century AD)*
Lost Gnostic writing, quoted by Epiphanius of
Salamis. *Gospel of Eve* was written at least a century
after the time of Jesus. Seemingly also known as
Gospel of Perfection.

Beginning after the fire in
Rome in AD 64, the Emperor
Nero harshly persecuted
Christians, killing significant
leaders such as Peter and Paul.
One of the motivations for
writing the Gospels may have
been the deaths—because of
Nero's persecution—of key
eyewitnesses of the life of Jesus.

■ *Gospel of the Hebrews* *(Christian writing, first century AD)*
Gospel of the Hebrews is truly a "lost Gospel"; it survives
only in quotations found in the writings of early
Christians. Many scholars believe *Gospel of the Hebrews*
represents an early, Aramaic summary of Jesus' life
from the apostle Matthew—a summary that eventually
became part of the document that now known as the
Gospel According to Matthew. Also known as *Gospel of
the Nazoreans.*

■ *Infancy Gospel of James* *(Christian writing, late second century AD)* An account,
supposedly written by James, of the life of Mary. According to this document,
Mary the mother of Jesus remained a virgin throughout her life.

■ *Acts of John* *(Docetic writing, late second century AD)* Supposed retelling of
events from the life of the apostle John. Some copies of this text include
comments that are *Docetic*—that is, they imply that Jesus Christ was not fully
human—but these comments are not present in every version. It is possible
that they were added later.

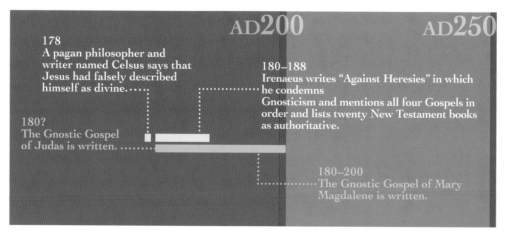

AD200   AD250

178
A pagan philosopher and
writer named Celsus says that
Jesus had falsely described
himself as divine.

180–188
Irenaeus writes "Against Heresies" in which
he condemns
Gnosticism and mentions all four Gospels in
order and lists twenty New Testament books
as authoritative.

180?
The Gnostic Gospel
of Judas is written.

180–200
The Gnostic Gospel of Mary
Magdalene is written.

■ *Gospel of Judas* *(Gnostic writing, late second century AD)* Supposed account of the life of Jesus in which Judas Iscariot is portrayed as a heroic figure, commanded by Jesus to act as the betrayer.

■ *Gospel of the Lord* *(Marcionite writing, mid-second century AD)* Alteration of the Gospel According to Luke, edited to fit Marcion's theology.

■ *Gospel of Mary* *(Gnostic writing, late second or early third century AD)* Although frequently called *Gospel of Mary Magdalene*, the text of this document never indicates *which* biblical Mary is the story's central character.

■ *Gospel of Matthias* *(Ancient writing, perhaps Gnostic, second century AD)* Lost document, known to many early Christians. This writing seems to have passed out of usage among Christians because (1) no clear evidence was available to suggest that the apostle Matthias actually wrote the book and (2) the book was used by heretical sects including the Gnostics.

■ *Gospel of Nicodemus* *(Forgery, fourth century AD)* Forgery that claimed to include Pontius Pilate's report to the emperor about Jesus. Also known as *Acts of Pilate*.

■ *Gospel, Oxyrhynchus* *(Christian writing, third century AD or earlier)* Not actually a Gospel but a tiny papyrus fragment from an unknown source, the "Oxyrhynchus Gospel" describes a confrontation between Jesus and the Pharisees. The events described in this fragment do not contradict any New Testament Gospels and seem to represent an expansion of the events described in Mark 7:1–23.

AD300   AD350

c. 350
Codex Vaticanus and Codex Sinaiticus, the oldest complete Bibles still in existence, were circulated.

332
Emperor Constantine orders production of 50 vellum Bibles.

325
The Council of Nicaea condemns Arius and his teachings and produces an early version of the Nicene Creed which clearly describes Jesus as God.

250–450
The rest of the Gnostic Nag Hammadi documents are written and circulated.

320
Arius claims Jesus is a created being and not God.

337 Constantine dies.

(Courtesy of CSNTM.org)

The first chapter of Mark's Gospel

■ *Gospel of Peter (Christian writing, second century* AD*)* Although familiar to many early Christians, this text was rejected as an authoritative account of the life of Jesus because (1) it could not be clearly connected to the apostle Peter and (2) some passages in the book could be misconstrued to suggest that Jesus wasn't fully human.

■ *Apocalypse of Peter (Christian writing, second century* AD*)* An apocalyptic text that circulated with *Gospel of Peter, Apocalypse of Peter* doesn't directly contradict any New Testament writings, but the book seems to have been written around AD 135, seventy years or so after the death of the apostle Peter.

■ *Coptic Apocalypse of Peter (Gnostic writing, late third century* AD*)* The *Coptic Apocalypse of Peter* clearly denied that Jesus had a physical body, declaring that "the one whose hands and feet they nailed to the cross [was] only a fleshly substitute."

■ *Gospel of Philip (Gnostic writing, third century* AD*)* Not actually a gospel but a collection of brief excerpts from other Gnostic writings, *Gospel of Philip* summarizes the views of the followers of the Gnostic leader Valentinus.

■ *Gospel of the Savior (Gnostic writing, early third century* AD*)* Not actually a Gospel but a few fragments from an ancient document known as Papyrus Berlin 22220, *Gospel of the Savior* seems to have been a Gnostic adaptation of *Gospel of Peter.* Also known as *Vision of the Savior.*

■ *Gospel of Thomas (Gnostic writing, mid-second century* AD*)* Not actually a Gospel, but a collection of sayings attributed to Jesus. Most sayings in *Gospel of Thomas* are similar to statements found in the New Testament Gospels. A few, however, seem to represent an early form of Gnosticism. Although some sayings in the book can be traced to the first century AD, the book did not emerge in its final form until the middle of the second century.

■ *Infancy Gospel of Thomas (Christian writing, mid-second century* AD*)* An account of the childhood of Jesus, supposedly written by the apostle Thomas. In this text, the boy Jesus uses his miraculous powers for his own benefit. The author's style of writing and his lack of knowledge about Jewish traditions suggest that the book was written in the mid-second century AD, long after the death of the apostle Thomas.

■ *Gospel of Truth* *(Gnostic writing, late second century AD)* Unearthed at Nag Hammadi in the 1940s, *Gospel of Truth* is a Gnostic retelling of the creation story and of the life of Jesus. According to Irenaeus of Lyons, a disciple of a Gnostic teacher named Valentinus wrote *Gospel of Truth*, also known as *Gospel of Valentinus*.

■ Why are so many people so enthralled by the "lost Gospels"?

Perhaps people long to believe that there's some knowledge or experience of Jesus Christ that isn't available in the New Testament Gospels—and, in some sense, they're correct. There *is* experience and knowledge of Jesus Christ that isn't available simply by reading the New Testament Gospels. But this knowledge and experience certainly is not available in the unreliable myths found in the "lost Gospels." The full knowledge and experience that our souls crave is available when we not only *read about* Jesus Christ but also *personally commit our lives to* Jesus Christ, the One in whom we can be "made complete" and through whom we can enter into fellowship with the God who gives us his love in "far greater abundance than any of us could ask or think" (Colossians 2:9; Ephesians 3:20).

Notes

1   See Bart Ehrman, *Lost Christianities* (New York: Oxford University Press, 2003) 3-5. Hereafter, *Lost Christianities* will be cited as *LC*, followed by the page numbers.

2   *MJ* 36.

3   Ehrman places the emergence of this principle later and summarizes it in this way: Authoritative texts had to be "ancient" (from the time of Jesus) and "apostolic" (from the first followers of Jesus or their associates) (*LC* 242-243). As Ehrman notes, two other standards came into play later, those of catholicity (widespread usage among Christians) and orthodoxy (agreement with other Scriptures). I would contend, though, that—for the earliest Christians—the categories of *orthodoxy, apostolicity,* and *antiquity* were not distinguishable. All three categories were rooted in the assumption that eyewitness testimony was authoritative.

4   Quoted in Eusebius, 3:39

5   It was, according to Eusebius, from these prophetesses that Papias received some stories about the apostles (Eusebius 3:39).

6   Muratorian Fragment.

7   Eusebius, 5:8.

8   *LC* 235.

9   Translated from "Muratorian Canon in Latin": Retrieved October 28, 2006, from http://www. earlychristianwritings.com/text/muratorian-latin.html.

10   Eusebius, 6:12.

11   See *LC* 16. The beginnings of blaming the crucifixion on the Jewish people can be seen in the trial before Pontius Pilate in *Gospel of Peter,* suggesting a date after the expulsion of Christians from the synagogues in the late first century AD

12   Eusebius, 6:12; cf. Tertullian of Carthage, *De Praescriptione Haereticorum,* 3:20-21: Retrieved October 28, 2006, from http://www.tertullian.org latin/de_praescriptione_haereticorum.html.

13   Eusebius, 5:8.

Author: Timothy Paul Jones, Ed.D

Excerpted material © 2007 Dr. Timothy Paul Jones. Excerpted from the book *Misquoting Truth: A Guide to the Fallacies of Bart Ehrman's Misquoting Jesus.* Published by InterVarsity Press (www.ivpress.com). All rights reserved. Reprinted by permission.

Visit the author on the Internet at: www.TimothyPaulJones.com

Special thanks to Craig L. Blomberg, Ph.D, Distinguished Professor of New Testament, Denver Seminary; Lew Whallon.

Early Lists of Authoritative Christian Writings

The Fragment of Muratori (mid-second century AD, Rome)	Codex Claromontanus (late third century AD, Egypt or North Africa)	Eusebius of Caesarea's Church History (early fourth century AD, Palestine and Asia Minor)	Letter of Athanasius (AD 367)

Accepted
Matthew
Mark
Luke
John
Acts
Romans
1 & 2 Corinthians
Galatians
Ephesians
Philippians
Colossians
1 & 2 Thessalonians
1 & 2 Timothy
Titus
Philemon
1 John
2 or 3 John (or both
   letters, counted as one)
Jude
Revelation
Wisdom of Solomon
[Epistle to the Hebrews
  and the letters of Peter
  not mentioned at all]
	Accepted
	Matthew
	Mark
	Luke
	John
	Acts
	Romans
	1 & 2 Corinthians
	Galatians
	Ephesians
	Philippians
	Colossians
	1 & 2 Thessalonians
	1 & 2 Timothy
	Titus
	Philemon
	Hebrews*
	James
	1 and 2 Peter
	1, 2, and 3 John
	Jude
	Revelation
		Accepted
		Matthew
		Mark
		Luke
		John
		Acts
		Romans
		1 & 2 Corinthians
		Galatians
		Ephesians
		Philippians
		Colossians
		1 & 2 Thessalonians
		1 & 2 Timothy
		Titus
		Philemon
		Hebrews
		1 Peter
		1 John
		Revelation*
			Accepted
			Matthew
			Mark
			Luke
			John
			Acts
			Romans
			1 & 2 Corinthians
			Galatians
			Ephesians
			Philippians
			Colossians
			1 & 2 Thessalonians
			1 & 2 Timothy
			Titus
			Philemon
			Hebrews
			James
			1 and 2 Peter
			1, 2, and 3 John
			Jude
			Revelation

Recognized but Questioned Apocalypse of Peter	**Recognized but Questioned** Apocalypse of Peter Epistle of Barnabas The Shepherd of Hermas Acts of Paul	**Recognized but Questioned** James Jude 2 Peter 2 and 3 John	**Recognized but Questioned**

Rejected
Laodiceans
Alexandrians
The Shepherd of
  Hermas
	Rejected
	(All other writings)
		Rejected
		Apocalypse of Peter
		Acts of Paul
		The Shepherd of Hermas
		Epistle of Barnabas
		Teaching of Twelve
		  Apostles
		Gospel of Peter
		Gospel of Thomas
		Gospel of Matthias
		Gospel of the
		  Hebrews
		Acts of Andrew
		Acts of John
			Rejected
			(All other writings)

> This chart shows that early Christians accepted the four Gospels according to Matthew, Mark, Luke, and John long before the critics claim, and that none of the so-called lost Gospels was *ever* accepted.

* indicates that this listing may have placed this writing in the list of questionable books

Look for Other Rose Bible Basics Books

Free, downloadable study guide at rose-publishing.com. *Click on "News & Info," then on "Downloads."*

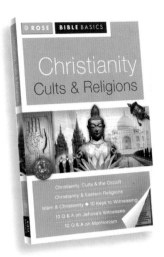

Christianity, Cults & Religions

Helps clarify differences between the beliefs and practices of various religions, cults, and new religious movements. Includes topics such as: Who is God? Who is Jesus Christ? What is salvation? What happens after death?

Contains comparisons of biblical Christianity with Anthroposophy, Bahá'í, Buddhism, Christian Science, Eastern mysticism, Hare Krishna, Hinduism, Islam, Jehovah's Witnesses, Judaism, Latter-day Saints/Mormons, Muslims, Nation of Islam, New age movement, Soka Gakkai International, Scientology (Dianetics), Theosophy, TM (Transcendental Meditation), Unification Church, Unity School, Wicca, Kabbalah, and more.

112 pages, 6 x 9-inch paperback.　ISBN: 9781596362024

Names of God and Other Bible Studies

Contains favorite Bible studies to use in small groups, church groups, and for individual study. Includes studies on the Names of God, Names of Jesus, Names of the Holy Spirit, Trinity, Ten Commandments, Lord's Prayer, Beatitudes, Fruit of the Spirit, and Armor of God. 112 pages. Includes color charts, illustrations, and photos throughout.

112 pages, 6 x 9-inch paperback.　ISBN: 9781596362031

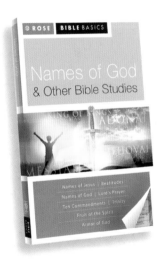

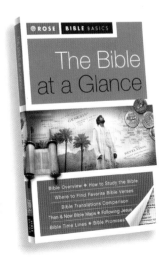

The Bible at a Glance

This introduction to basic Bible knowledge contains: a Bible overview summarizing each book of the Bible in 100 words or less, a Bible time line comparing Bible history and world history side by side, an introduction to studying the Bible, Then & Now Bible Maps, where to find favorite Bible verses, Bible promises, the basics of the Christian life, and a Bible translations comparison chart.

112 pages, 6 x 9-inch paperback.　ISBN: 9781596362000

Other Rose Publishing Books

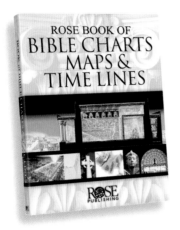

Rose Book of Bible Charts, Maps & Time Lines
Dozens of popular Rose Publishing Bible charts, maps, and time lines in one spiral-bound book. Reproduce up to 300 copies of any chart free of charge.

192 pages. Hardcover.   ISBN-13: 9781596360228

Deluxe "Then and Now" Bible Maps
Book with CD-ROM!
See where Bible places are today with "Then and Now" Bible maps with clear plastic overlays of modern cities and countries. This deluxe edition comes with a CD-ROM that gives you a JPG of each map to use in your own Bible material as well as PDFs of each map and overlay to create your own handouts or overhead transparencies. PowerPoint fans can create their own presentations with these digitized maps.

Hardcover. ISBN-13: 9781596361638

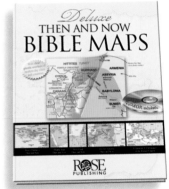

Rose Book of Bible & Christian History Time Lines
Six thousand years and 20 feet of time lines in one hard-bound cover! This unique resource allows you to easily store and reference two time lines in book form. These gorgeous time lines printed on heavy chart paper, can also be slipped out of their binding and posted in a hallway or large room for full effect.
• The 10-foot Bible Time Line compares Scriptural events with world history and Middle East history. Shows hundreds of facts; includes dates of kings, prophets, battles, and key events.
• The 10-foot Christian History Time Line begins with the life of Jesus and continues to the present day. Includes key people and events that all Christians should know. Emphasis on world missions, the expansion of Christianity, and Bible translation in other languages. These two time lines are connected end-to-end to form one long teaching aid.

Hardcover. ISBN-13: 9781596360846